Pampering
Pleasures

*101 Refreshing 'Me-Time' Rituals
For Your Mind, Body, & Spirit*

Ella Patterson

Global One is Division of Knowledge Concepts Systems

Ella Patterson

Pampering Pleasures
101 Refreshing 'Me-Time' Rituals for Your Mind, Body, & Spirit
Global One is A Division of Knowledge Concepts Publications
P. O. Box 973 * Cedar Hill, Texas 75106 -0973
Copyright © 2010 Ella Patterson

Library of Congress has cataloged this edition as follows
Patterson, Ella © 2010

Ella Patterson
Pampering Pleasures:
101 Refreshing 'Me-Time' Rituals For Your Mind, Body, & Spirit
Ella Patterson - 1st. Edition,
1st printing 2010
p. cm.

1. Health. 2. Mind. 3. Body 4.Sexuality. 5. Women. 6. Relationships.
7. Sex-Esteem 8.Resource. 9. Psychology. 10. Education

I. Ella Patterson. II. Title.

This book includes *Questionnaire, *Resources for Women, *Reference Books, Index, *Helpful Websites for Women, and *Order Form

Printed and bound in United States of America
Knowledge Concepts Publications
C/O Book Orders Dept. (USA), Inc.
P O Box 973 - Cedar Hill, TX. 75106
Phone: 972-223-1558   Fax: 214-988-2864

ISBN: 1-884331-45-9   CIP: 95 - 94105
LCCN: 2006902470   SAN: 257 - 6163

10 9 8 7 6 5 4 3 2

✍ USA $14.95
CAN $19.95

More Books by Ella

Will The Real Women ... Please Stand Up!
Will The Real Men ... Please Stand Up!
Relationship Quickies
Stupid Things Men Should Never Say To Women
Pick A Better Partner
1001 Reasons to Think Positive
Successful Things Women Do
Moving In the Right Direction
Higher Expectations
Lifelines
Smart Moves
Heated Pleasures
Pampering Pleasures
Sexual Healing
The Potent Woman

Submit wholesale orders to:
Knowledge Concepts Systems
Book Orders Dept. (USA)
P O Box 973 - Cedar Hill, TX.   75106
Phone: 972-854-1824

Ella Patterson

pamper in Dutch is koesteren, troetelen, vertroetelen
pamper in French is mignoter, mignotons, dorloter, choyer, mignotez
pamper in Spanish is mimar
pamper in Swedish is klema bort

Dedication

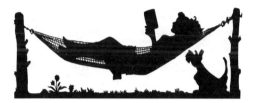

This book is dedicated to women who really want to rediscover the joy and magic of pampering.

Here's What People Are Saying ...
About Pampering Pleasures

Because of this pampering book and its inspirational pampering tips' I started giving MYSELF gifts. I bought my own birthday gift this year and loved doing it. It was fun to know that I was getting JUST what I wanted!!!
~ Betty Artis, DeSoto, TX

This book is making me feel like I'm taking a nice relaxing trip. Some of these things I thought I knew, but since I started reading Pampering Pleasures I'm learning so much more. This book is a woman's ENTRÉE to growth, wisdom and knowledge.
~ Venita McFadden, Ft. Worth, TX

I can see how this book will give women additional reasons to take care of themselves. It has helped open my mind to great times, and great experiences. It has helped me make small, but important adjustments in my attitude, scheduling, environments and pampering techniques.
~ Juanna Johnson, Lancaster, TX

This is a handbook of essential information about how to live by your own pampered light. I love it!
~ Carol Murray, Dallas, TX

The things I do when I decide to pamper myself are... I go shopping, have my nails and toes done and then I hang out at places where I can have nothing but my private moments.
~ Alieya Strain, Lancaster, TX

Pampering Pleasures

"When I am pampered every experience of my life is somehow new again.
My senses are more acute than ever before.
I find pleasure in the smallest tasks,
No matter how routine life is.
There is a place of healing inside me now;
where I feel as if I'm standing on top of the world.
I feel completely sure of myself.
I finally can say I love me again.
I am now feeling the flow of the currents
and I realize I am not moving against them.
I stand in the center of my own life,
ready to move in a direction that is fitting,
fulfilling and functional.
I am now a pampered woman."

~ Ella Patterson

Contents

 Warning:

This is a *'girlfriends'* book!

A Note from the Author

I can remember when I got the idea to write this book. I needed information that focused more on pampering pleasures instead of beauty and cosmetics products.

Self-pampering is the perfect example of a woman's desire to bring self-love to the forefront. It is stimulating, soothing, and also rewarding. For many it has proven to be the do-it-yourself way for relaxation and self-care.

During many of my girl's night outs workshops I am barraged with questions. How do I start? Where do I do it? How do I handle the children when I need some personal time to myself? How do I get my lover to pamper me more in the ways that I like to be pampered without hurting his feelings? And how do I give more pampering pleasures to the people I care about?

Women want and need a guide to help them successfully navigate the unsure waters of self-love, self-care and self-pampering. We have been conditioned to think that self-love is selfish, but isn't it just as important as self-care? I believe it is. The need to love and care for yourself is a major necessity for any woman who wants to live a successfully happy and long life. Pampering is the best form of female maintenance.

Here, in this book are activities that women can do to bring comfort to their minds, bodies and spirits. Offered in this book are some of the most basic pampering pleasures. Pampering is my way of leaving the world behind.

This is a practical book filled with specific pampering techniques. I was the guinea pig. I refined my craft and sharpened my knowledge so that I could communicate everything to you. I'm sharing many personal experiences in these pages and letting you know every pampering technique I've tried. It's not just my story, but also the story of many of my clients with more than a hundred spa techniques.

I hope this book will help you discover the 'you' who you've always wanted to be. I hope this book will help you understand the importance of creating your own pampering pleasures too. It is a girlfriend's book so it carries a very special message for women who want and need to be pampered. It will make a valuable difference in your life.

May this book bring much needed love and pampering to your lifestyle.

~ Ella P

Preface

For more than a half century, Ella Patterson's signature blend of comfort, style and sensuality has been a source of inspiration in homes of her family, friends and co-workers. Now in homes across America Ella will share her pampering secrets to help you create sensual atmospheres, luxurious, refreshing spaces that are as beautiful as they are practical and as distinctive as the rest of your home.

This essential guide offers imaginative design, decorating tips and pampering pleasures any woman can call her own. The ideas offered are easy ideas exclusively for the sensuous woman. In Pampering Pleasures, chapters devoted to everything from setting the stage for pampering, why pampering is needed, indulging in me-time rituals, pampering principles and how you can create a place you can call your space. From strengthening your senses, stocking your pampering pantry, essential oils, pampering your partner, restorative rituals for your mind, body, and spirit to guiding you along as you host a girl's night in pamper party. You'll discover ways to enjoy retreats away from home to creating an environment at home that's full of nurturing and ambience. Tours that help you create your sensual bedroom and over 150 'Me Time' Rituals that help you become the Diva you were meant to be.

Included are types of spas that pamper so you'll always get it right when you need to get away from it all. Quick reference guides throughout the book that will make it easy to choose ideas to apply to your own home. With friendly, straight forward advice and hundreds of ideas, *Pampering Pleasures* is the definite source book for 'me-time-rituals.

Word of Advice

Enjoy this book and its benefits. Open your mind and begin to explore the contents of this book and you will not only enjoy what you read, you'll gain new knowledge as you began to understand the real message. I'm hoping this book will be a wonderful luxury for you. Having it in your possession should already make you feel special.

Embrace This Information

In order to embrace yourself fully you have to first, give yourself permission to move forward with these personal pleasures. Embrace this information by learning how to put it to good use. This will help you make positive adjustments in your life.

At times, I will share principle information and explain it in detail - other times I will share small tips and techniques that make a huge difference in your life. You'll come to understand why it's so important to indulge and have fabulous 'me-time', and as you do you'll discover who you are and what you like. As you begin to renew your mind and spirit you'll notice a wonderful transformation that allows you to reap the benefits in love and life.

There's more to life than having everything.

Introduction

This Book is Rare, but Needed

In this chapter you'll learn how to use this book in the best possible way.

With *Pampering Pleasures* most any woman can feel good about herself. It's rare to find a book such as this one - one that provides quality advice on how to administer pampering and wonderful stress-free indulgences.

Each of these chapters will help you recapture the joy of life's simple pleasures, but before we get too deep into how good pampering feels, let's first discuss why *any* woman would need pampering pleasures and why this information is important to women.

This Is a Girlfriend Book

Here's your invitation to become immersed in simple indulgences of pampering pleasures. I pray that along the way this book will help you adopt a wholesome and healthy attitude toward your own needs.

While many of the pampering tips in this book are obvious to some they are quite absent to others. I suggest you keep these treats in mind when striving for self-love, renewal and healing. It is my experience that these pampering treats will add years to any woman's life; which makes them well worth knowing. Because this is a very personal book for women, I suggest women keep it in their pampering pantry - near their pampering supplies.

This is a book you must do! It is a 'self-help' kind of book. It's filled with simple, easy-to-do techniques that will help you feel good inside and outside. Most importantly this book will help any woman become the pampered woman she is meant to be. If you really indulge and make it a natural part of your life it will do many other great things for you too. It will help…

1. Raise your self-esteem and make you feel better.
2. Create important moments of self-love.
3. Enhance and enrich your life.
4. Improve your mental state.
5. Bring your inner Diva out.
6. Make you feel appreciated and special.
7. Empower you to refine and improve yourself.
8. Create commitment to your spiritual wholeness.
9. Turn on your inner light and recharge your inner battery.
10. Enhance your inner and outer beauty.

Knowing how much this book will help you should ease some of your worries and concerns about why you need a book like this. You should also know that this is a purpose driven book that can motivate even the most doubtful woman.

To Help You Follow This Book

Here are some helpful tips on how to enjoy the wonderful pampering pleasures of this book. As you read - here's what I suggest: try one or more of the pampering selections each day. If you want, you can read this book in its entirety before trying any of the treats. If you find something particularly delicious and you don't have enough time to indulge in it; try another treat; something that requires shorter time - then come back to the longer indulgences at a later time. To start your very own personal pampering regiment let's get started.

RELAX: Find your special place; somewhere quiet, stress free, and comfortable, so that you can read this book uninterrupted. Give yourself a few moments to relax completely before you begin reading. Take a deep breath, get comfortable and clear your mind.

READ: Read each insight carefully and concentrate without feeling rushed or hurried. Get a full understanding, and then share the insights with a friend or your partner.

THINK: Spend a few moments to analyze and consider what you read. Repeat or paraphrase it out loud to yourself.

Understand the importance of each pampering treat. Know that each insight can be personalized to fit your personal pampering need.

APPLY: Welcome each insight and put them into practice. Use them daily in your own life. Think of ways to strengthen your relationship with self and others as you use them.

This book is your path to unconditional self-love, joy and personal satisfaction. The pampering pleasures in this book will help you express outwardly the joy you feel inwardly.

You will get to experience and understand that self-love is your path to loving others and pampering is your path to pleasurable self-love.

If you love yourself and what you do, then you'll never really lose.

~ Ellaism

1

Setting the Stage for Pampering

In this chapter you'll learn the most positive ways to put yourself first.

B efore you read further into *Pampering Pleasures* there's one more thing you should do. Release any feelings of anxiety you're having because of life's pressures and give yourself permission to feel good about your new journey. Relax your mind, body and spirit; because this is not the time to think about any of your problems or disappointments. This is your time – time for self-indulgence and feel good moments. Lift your chin, raise your head to the heavens and let's take a journey toward improvement.

With all the responsibilities women have it's a wonder there's time to apply any kind of pampering. You probably lead a very hectic life … always on the move trying to meet deadlines, having endless meetings, appointments and nonstop duties from one minute to the next.

I understand your dilemma because I experience many of these same things. Along with emails, phone calls, and on-going projects that I must complete I often feel overwhelmed, not knowing what to do and when to do it. Sometimes I get frustrated, flustered and beat down by it all. With a business to run, bills to pay, a home to take care of, employees to pay, and contacts to make; the 'to-do's' never seem to slow down.

I know that you can relate to those times when there just doesn't seem to be enough time to do all the things you have to do. It probably feels like the more things you have to do the more there's left to do.

If you think back to simpler times you'll recall as a little girl you were the one being taken care of. You were groomed and prepared for luxurious womanhood and along this journey you realized that one day you'll have to do things for yourself just to keep up. Taking care of yourself is the natural order of things, and you have to do things that will help you look good, feel good and be good to yourself. You have to remind yourself that you are number one and you should be at the top of your pampering list.

Putting Yourself at the Top of Your List

Usually during personal crisis, turmoil or after listening to your inner voice you wonder if it's time to reevaluate your life and decide whether the work you are doing is your life's mission. You'll wonder if you're getting all you can or being all you can be or if it's worth your time and effort to keep going the way you're going. You'll probably ask yourself, "Am I getting any return on my investment of time and energy? "How much of my life have I handed over to others who aren't worthy?"

You'll finally start understanding that there's more to life than your career, or your business.

Maybe years of conditioning have taught you to let others depend on you for fulfillment. It might come in the disguise of businesses that are all about their mission statement so that they can get what they want in order to achieve their goals.

Maybe you end up investing too much of your time and energy in things that don't make you feel good about your life, or you find that you are desperately searching for something that cannot be found in the place you presently are. You want a better life and even more than that - you deserve to have one.

As you grow and start to live your life, your mind, body and spirit become challenged by your daily activities. You are bombarded with society's portrayal of who you should be and after all of this you feel like you're not taking care of yourself, not to mention that you feel unappreciated. You actually feel neglected, which further diminishes your ability to love yourself with the zest and attitude you had as a child.

How do you stop the madness? How do you end the cycle of neglect? How do you remain solid as a woman? How do you keep it all together? How do you place yourself at the top of your own list?

It all starts here. Today is a new beginning. Today you stop the perpetration of 'busyness makes you important'. Your busyness does not give you a healthy frame of mind nor does it give you good health, peace of mind or self-fulfillment. Today you begin pampering yourself. Today you develop an intimate relationship with yourself. Today your personal renewal begins.

Pampering Pleasures assist you in uncovering the things you like and want. This is your guide to finding your path to self-love, and for those who already know what self-love is - it will help you get reacquainted with yourself and reclaim your spirit. Pampering is so necessary for inner growth and self-nurturing, which is sacred to every woman who indulges in it.

When Was The Last Time You Relaxed?

When was the last time you totally relaxed in the peacefulness of your own home? When was the last time you experienced complete silence... no radio, music, television, conversation or telephone ringing - simply complete silence? When? Most women are so busy they can't remember. Your inner voice may be telling you to slow down, but you are so busy that you cannot hear it. Maybe you have become disconnected to what your true self wants. When you need to relax and you know that you need it desperately you have an *"I'll do it some other time attitude."* You act as if your well-being and health is negotiable and because consistent self-pampering is healthy your love for self is interrelated.

How You Can Pamper Yourself

Do you find yourself taking a back seat to your children, husband, family or job? Do you feel that if you pamper yourself you're neglecting others? Have you ever just wanted a few minutes to yourself, where all you do is focus on nobody except you? Stress no more about these things. Once you understand that stress is a very real problem you'll also understand that pampering and relaxation helps you coast through stress. They usually go hand in hand – stress causes you to seek the relaxation so-to-speak. It's a fact that women are more susceptible to stress-related symptoms and diseases, so it's important that you learn how to pamper yourself.

So the bigger question is how do you learn to pamper yourself? It isn't as hard as you might think. Let's begin now. Lie this book down and for the next five minutes' walk through your home and do some simple observing.

Cut the ringer to the phone off, silence any alarm clocks that might ring. Turn the television off and go to your favorite room. For the next fifteen minutes don't speak or talk to anyone. Be still. Enjoy the quietness and embellish the peacefulness that surrounds you. Close your eyes and free your mind of any obstructive thoughts. Meditate, talk to God or quietly think good thoughts. Do nothing for fifteen minutes… I mean it! **Do Nothing**!

After your fifteen-minutes of meditation find your favorite chair and relax with your favorite drink. Get comfortable and enjoy being you. It's that simple. You have just indulged in your first pampering pleasure.

By three methods we may learn wisdom: First, by reflection,
which is noblest; Second, by imitation, which is easiest; and third
by experience, which is the bitterest.
~ Confucius

2

Why Pampering Is Needed

In this chapter you will learn how to add yourself to your list of things to do

E veryone deserves time where they can relax and do things or have things done that make them feel like they're being taken care of. We all need a few minutes to soak in a hot bath without interruptions. We need to enjoy our moments of relaxation without being asked to fulfill the needs of someone else.

Pampering yourself is okay? Give yourself permission to take some downtime. It is not selfish, over-indulgent, opulent, excessive or self-centered. Quite frankly, it's necessary for everyone to spend some personal time taking care of their mind, body and spirit.

Everything and everyone needs attention; so much so, that *you* are usually the last person on your list of people to take care of. There's the family, the pet, the job, the kitchen, the bathroom, the home, the garden, the chores, the meals, etc. What about you? Are you the least taken care of sometimes? If you are I'm sure you understand why personal pampering is so necessary? It's important that *you* moments of pampering feel peaceful. These moments might not happen every hour, but maybe you can do it for yourself once every week or at least twice a month.

The one thing you must understand is: No one, not even your favorite person will hand you pampering pleasures on a silver platter each time you feel the need for them. They will never be able to give you the life that you dreamed of having either. It won't happen unless you make it happen on your own. So why wait on someone else to do it for you? Pick up your body, get out there and start. This is your time to do for you - what you would like to have done. It's time to spoil yourself and make a big deal out of you. And guess what; you can do it regularly for no reason at all. Your pampering times are the times that you spoil yourself rotten in big or little ways just because.

Your Inner Diva is longing for and worthy of being pampered. Go ahead fuss over yourself. Relax and do lots of positive things for yourself. Once in a while do absolutely whatever you desire to do. Don't think about it, just be free and do whatever makes you feel spoiled rotten. And don't forget to create a personal place where you can go and feel that all is right in your world.

Before you move forward, let's figure out what's important to you. How can you affirm a new attitude about your own pampering pleasures? For this exercise jot down your own beliefs of what self-indulgence means to you.

What Are Your Existing Beliefs About Self -Pampering?

1. _____

2. _____

3. _____

4. _____

5. _____

Okay, now that that's done, let's work to change any negative views you have about self-indulgence. Repeat the following affirmations at least five times and believe what you say.

1. I will pamper myself for my own sense of peace.
2. I will gain a better understanding of pampering pleasures.
3. I will commit to pampering myself.
4. I will work to incorporate pampering into my daily life.
5. I will not allow people, places, things or circumstances to disrupt my pampering pleasures time.

Can you feel your old attitudes about self-indulgence changing yet? Are you able to pat yourself on the back and say, "I am okay and I deserve my pampering moments?" When you accept the fact that self-indulgent pampering is okay you begin to get more comfortable with your own ideas.

The principles found in this book are universal. They are pampering guidelines that will help you get in touch with your Inner Diva, that special part of you that you save for yourself. These pampering pleasures are here for you to indulge, explore and evolve with. They are the essence of who you really are. They transcend culture, time, age and time.

Self-love is a part of who you are, but you must get in tune with it each and every day in order for it to be the most beneficial.

3

Understanding Pampering Pleasures

In this chapter you'll gain ideas on how to incorporate pampering

pleasures.

L et's take a few minutes to get a sense of what pampering really is and what is should be. Some of the most indulgent activities a woman can get involved with when relaxing, distressing or releasing are in her home. Maybe you're the kind of woman that takes a shower instead of a bath because it requires less time to get the job done. Because our society chooses to do things quicker - lengthy pampering rituals have fallen by the wayside. You have a choice whether you want short or lengthy pampering rituals. To incorporate your very own pampering pleasures here's how you do it.

1. **Know Who You Are.** Get acquainted with yourself. Know what you like, dislike, want and don't want. Become your own best critic and friend.

2. **Love Who You Are.** You have to love who you are if want to know what you need. Love every bump, mole, scar and imperfection. Love all of yourself every day in every way.

3. **Respect and Appreciate Yourself.** Hold yourself to the highest esteem possible. Never think badly of yourself and always find a way to boost your own spirit.

4. **Nourish your body and soul.** Stay healthy in spirit, body and mind. Keep your body healthy.

5. **Keep your mind healthy.** Think good thoughts and take hateful or negative thoughts from your mind. Replace them with good messages.

6. **Treat your body like it's a temple.** Because there are no replacements for your body, you should treat it with special concern and admiration. It's yours so treat it good and it will be good to you.

7. **Remain connected to a higher source.** Be sure to include prayer and mediation in your daily regiment.

8. **Listen to your inner voice.** Don't ignore yourself. When your Inner Diva is speaking to you – listen. She usually has good things to say to you.

9. **Pamper yourself with confidence.** Feed your spirit with positive nurturing. Get rid of the chips on your shoulder and reasons to be angry. Pamper yourself every day.

10. **Relax and release.** Clear your mind each day. It will provide harmony and balance in your life from a positive perspective.

4

Indulging In Me-Time Rituals

Even if your busyness tells you that you can't afford to indulge in pampering, know that you can't afford not to

Many years ago, I wrote myself a note that read, *'Indulge more in the things I enjoy.'* It was a personal mission that I find ways to enjoy my life, pamper myself and seek lifestyle pleasures that made me happy on a daily basis. My only objective was to experience fun ways to indulge in the kinds of pampering pleasures that would make me feel good on my inside and outside. Of course during this revelation I was convinced that I needed to take more time for myself. I needed to pamper me. I needed to indulge.

We All Deserve To Indulge

We all deserve to pamper ourselves. We deserve to indulge in those kinds of things that make us feel special when we can take a few moments to ourselves where we won't be bothered.

My favorite me-time ritual is while soaking in a nice bubble bath. Here, I can feel free to enjoy a private glass of wine while resting my head on a bath pillow. Sometimes I like to soak quietly with a bunch of lit candles surrounding my tub while listening to my favorite music, and then there are times when I like to cuddle in my favorite chair with a girlfriend kind of book while sipping my favorite cup of tea.

I believe in my soul that every woman deserves the luxury of self-indulgence. I think we all need to indulge ourselves from time to time.

Most every woman who walks the tight rope of life feels pressured or either short on her personal time. We all know at least one woman who spends more time pampering her loved ones than she does herself. Take me; I use to be the last one to get pampered, the last one to get attention and the last one on my own pampering list.

Because of this I decided to do something positive about it. I gave myself wonderful moments of pampering treats that made me feel good about myself. I also decided that I could do it in a way that it wouldn't feel selfish or neglectful to others.

It was time for me to feel special, so I went on a journey to find the best 'me-time' rituals that could happen for me every month, every week or maybe even every day without spending a lot of money.

We Have To Do It for Ourselves

As women; we have to understand that no one can really pamper us better than we can pamper ourselves and no one can treat us as good as we should treat ourselves. No one can as provide the personal self-indulgent luxuries in our daily regiment as we can for ourselves. It will only happen when we make it happen for ourselves. We are responsible for our own happiness and we can't get caught up in thinking our pampering moments are someone else's duties or problems. We not only neglect ourselves when we think this way, we also fail to bring happiness to our own lives.

Instead of waiting on your man to pamper you or your children to spoil you, why not do it for yourself? Don't wait to be asked - just do it. Tell yourself that it's okay to indulge in pampering. It's okay to reward yourself for a job well done. Sometimes, it's as simple as ordering caviar instead of tuna fish. You can do that can't you?

Discover Your Inner Diva

I suppose you're wondering where do your personal pampering pleasures come from. They come from your Inner Diva.

Your Inner Diva is the part of you that makes you desire special treatment and it makes you feel unique and different from all of the women around you. It also makes you feel worthy of living a pampered lifestyle. It's *"that thing"* that makes you want to be more than an ordinary woman.

It also lets you know and understand that your physical self is by no means the totality of who you are. It does, however reflect that you are a unique spiritual being of extraordinary beauty and importance.

You are a Diva!

When you understand and see yourself as a Diva you treat yourself as if you are cared for and live your life as if it were a part of your grand design. You are rewarded with an unmistakable radiance that comes from deep within and it shows from your inside - outward.

You can think of *"that thing"* it is thought of as your outward expression; your charisma, grace, class, and poise. When you have it, your eyes really are windows to the soul. When you have it your smile can put anyone at ease. You recognize the inner light. That light that the people who care about you already see and you open the channels for even more of that light to express itself. You possess the kind of radiance that can light up a room, light up your life and give you the kind of beauty that pampering pleasures will casily enhance.

Give Your Inner Spirit a Boost

Be realistic about what you feel is a pampered life. We all want great moments of luxury, indulgence and pampering. But don't go overboard with your quest to be a pampered woman. Going out and making a lot of bills buying things that will make you feel pampered is a little ridiculous. The kind of pampering I'm talking about is those indulgences that give your inner spirit a boost.

I have a friend who's on every television show that's broadcasted. She's a model and looks perfect all the time, but if you were to visit her home you'd ask yourself what tornado hit it? I have to laugh when I think about how much of a pack rat she is, but the public sees her as the Goddess of looks. Yes, she looks good and is a great friend, but her home is so unorganized and tacky that I shutter to think what's buried under all that mess. Her home isn't picture perfect even though she looks like she is.

The beauty of this story is she doesn't even care. She doesn't let it get her down. It probably bothers me more than it does her and her inner spirit is so high she doesn't think twice about how much of a space junky she is. It only leaves me with one thing say, *"To each her own."*

What Kind of Day Is It For You?

There will be days that you feel good and some days you will feel bad, but there will also be days when you need a little extra pampering in your life to feel loved and needed. There will be days when you want to feel more special than any other day. It might be the very day you decide to get a full body massage, or a new and different hair-do, or maybe it's the day you'll spend quiet time at home, pampering yourself from head to toe. What kind of day is it for you? Whatever kind of day it is will help you determine what kind of pampering you need to indulge in.

Find a Role Model

Find a woman that you consider your role model and study how she indulges in the luxuries of pampering. Is there any one thing she does that you want to happen for you? Does she display the assets of grace and assuredness? Is she stylish, have a signature look and seem to have life by the horns. If so, learn her tricks of the trade. Learn how you can indulge yourself in grand style while remaining on your budget. Copy her style without duplicating it. By this I mean take bits and pieces of what you like about her and then add your own personal attributes to create your own signature style.

Spend Quality Time Indulging

In Pampering Pleasures you will find page after page of inexpensive tips, treats and techniques to make your humdrum everyday life more indulgent, caring and worthwhile. Pampering pleasures are about you finding fun ways to spend quality time pampering and creating a private world of indulgence for yourself. This book will give you simple ways to: feel good, look good and be good to yourself.

Always make the time, find the time and cherish the time you set aside for pampering. Don't allow your pampering time to feel rushed or limited. Plan it out so the real benefits of pampering take you on a journey of enhanced pampering. This is your time to enrich your life. This is your time to do something nice for yourself. This is your time to slow down and enjoy life's rewards.

The Beauty of Pampering

Many of us who are otherwise intelligent, sensitive, passionate adults feel like complete idiots when it comes to pampering ourselves. We want to be pampered and healed, but we don't quite know how to incorporate it in our daily lives. We think spending money, buying food and new clothes or material things is a great way to pamper ourselves, but it actually isn't the *best* way to indulge.

We want pampering that feels good to our minds, bodies and souls. We want refreshing rituals that offer us a taste of the divine. The beauty of this book is that it makes the secrets of pampering common knowledge. It offers women a manual for navigating the pampering process by using their very own pampering rituals.

I hope that you find small and big ways to indulge in pampering. I encourage you to try the upcoming soothing me-time rituals that make you feel special.

Innocent, Yet Pleasurable Treats

With pampering rituals at your fingertips, you can experience the fullness of living without wasting time or money. When you feel the need to recapture a lost dream, gain a fresh perspective, or experience a pleasure - these treats and retreats are great ways to create innocent escapes of your own. They're great for your mind, body and spirit.

Starting today don't simply stop and smell the roses, smell fresh air, roll in the leaves, take deep refreshing breathes, sing in the shower, walk in the rain, and by all means laugh out loud. Rediscover the simple indulges like going bare feet, listening to rain drops, taking a midday snooze, or hanging out with your best friend - sharing beautiful moments of pampering.

Pampering pleasures motivates us to be creative thinkers and positive problems solvers. They relax our bodies, and our souls. Pleasurable experiences have proven to be the most significant ingredient in a long, healthy effective life because they promote the release of endorphins and boost our immunity.

Laugh at the clouds, smile at the sun and wink at the moon.

5

Portal to Pleasurable Pampering... Enter Here

Pampering pleasures helps a woman achieve a relaxed and balanced mood that nurtures her life and well-being.

I f you take time and think about your very beginning; you'll realize there were many pleasures. Your life and your very existence here on earth have been filled with pleasurable moments. For a moment think of the times your pleasures have pulled you in the direction you needed to go. From conception to your birth you are a form of unified pleasure. And as you grew into your adulthood you found ways to indulge in the kinds of pleasures you believed were filled with exploration, and rejuvenation. You probably have already had some of the kinds of pleasures that most women long to experience.

Your very body pulsates with pleasures as it discovers the wonders of self-love and self-indulgence? With this in mind how can you deny your body the pampering it needs? How can you call your desire for passion and pleasure anything, but healthy when everyday of your life you need it? How can you call your body anything, but God's wonder when your heart beats with loyalty twenty-four hours a day, every day and every year of your life? How can you think of your lungs as anything, but a miracle as they religiously drink in all the air that you need from morning to night? And what could be more indulgent than your brain jubilantly functioning on the level that it does - bringing knowledge, and the tenacity to succeed in every thought and pleasure you can conceive?

It may seem that some of these pampering pleasures are as natural as breathing and being alive. The same pleasures that drive you toward a state of well-being are also your essential nature - not just physically, but spiritually. It is what allows you to give birth to yourself over and over again. Each new pleasure, each new beginning, each inner renewal, each personal transformation, each change of direction is fueled by your desire to pamper yourself and to find truth, happiness and freedom.

Each time you choose to change, grow and improve, you are choosing to act from the inner core of self. It's your pampering indulgence that throughout your life will be your saving grace. For these pleasures will keep your spirit high and keep you going toward your dreams when you feel like giving up. Your self-care, self-love and self-indulgence will keep you traveling on the right path to inner renewal. Ultimately it will lead you to the destiny that you can already hear calling to you from within your own heart.

What Do You Know About Yourself?

Even though some women would like to say they don't need *Pampering Pleasures*, the truth is - they do - we all do!

We need these rituals because it presents an authentic healing experience for us -- an experience that helps us discover who we are. It helps us understand why it's so important for us to know more about ourselves than anyone else on this earth.

Who you are is *your* authentic self -- the self that God meant for you to be. Discovering *what you know about yourself* is the core of your emotional and spiritual self. If every woman would take the initiative and get to know herself in deeper and more personal ways the world would be filled with happier women.

I challenge every woman to 'know who you are.' I challenge you to love yourself enough to pamper yourself everyday of your life.

Rather than mark this celebration of women with a collection of antidotes, this book is a representation of how to be a better woman, 'a pampered woman' -- and it contributes bits of wisdom that have worked for centuries.

I don't know if you really understand this, but *"Wisdom is a continuing process."* It's similar to a woman's life cycle -- constantly growing, changing and forever improving.

You Can Become A Pampered Woman Too!

One morning I woke up to the realization that, I have become a happy woman, experiencing more pampered moments of contentment than moments of unfulfilled distress. Feeling authentic, confident and joyful

I began writing *Pampering Pleasures* more from a pampered lifestyle point of view than a momentary thrill point of view. This is a healing lifestyle book for women who want, as I do, to live by their own pampered light.

The book you're now reading bears no resemblance to the book I first began writing or to the book my agent and editor expected. While I wrote for ten years, I gathered information and interviewed women.

Pampering Pleasures has undergone an extraordinary metamorphosis, just as I have. On a different page every morning I would write something that helped me retreat from my busy schedule to become an emotionally, pampered women. I was on an intimate search for wholeness. When I began writing this book, it started out as a woman's guide to sexual fulfillment. Then something hit me and I felt more of a need to write about how women can pamper themselves by way of 'me-time rituals without the stress why they did it. Because I have written books and given professional advice on sex and sexuality I went a different direction with this book and began to write more about pampering oneself than sexing one's lover.

My girl's night out's have become 'girls night in' and my bubble baths have become pampering-body-rituals. My personal get-a-ways are now moments of serenity in a special space that I call my 'private place.' No one is more surprised than I am.

As *Pampering Pleasures* evolved from having more sex with your lover into having more authentic healing time for one's self, I began to barely recognize the woman I once was. *Pampering Pleasures* has provided me the opportunity to experience daily moments of epiphanies, find the sacred moments in the ordinary, discover the spiritual in the questionable, and enter moments of self-gratifying pleasure.

Everyday of my life is a new learning experience and a source for reflection, revelation, and reconnection: I now appreciate my hot flashes, mood swings, deadlines, dirty linen, allergies, grocery shopping, broken finger nails, unpolished toes, bad hair days, pampering, shopping, friends, men, children, family, unexpected phones calls, uninvited guests, and even the thirty pounds I keep swearing I'm going to loose.

Pampering Pleasures has also reminded me of what 'me-time' retreats are. It has shown me how to spend quiet and private moments reveling in wonderful pampering pleasures. It has given me the awareness that authentic female celebrations are the most personal form of being a woman. Everyday life has become my pampering pleasures.

Writing *Pampering Pleasures* has confirmed the reason I was at first - so unsure about how to write this book. I wasn't living the real life of a pampered woman - a life for which I was created. I try to now!

At least I can now recognize who I am and what makes me authentically happy. I don't have a million dollars in the bank, but I now realize what it takes to make me feel happy. My quiet time in a special place has become as essential as breathing. Everyday I make the choice of what I will and will not settle for. I decide with whom, when and where I will spend my time.

At the heart of this *Pampering Pleasures* Journey is an earthshaking awakening that has utterly changed how I view my life's mission and the time I spend taking care of myself. Knowing who I am and what I want in life is my pampered pleasure. This book has become my *pampered soul made visible.*

Why Some Women Feel Neglected

Even though women are working dillingently to incorporate more pampering moments in their schedules, they often feel there are just not enough hours in the day. This causes women to regret what they're feeling and in turn reject the very idea of doing nice things for themselves.

A woman often feels alone in her quest to find ways to be true to herself. In many cases she feels neglected by the person she cares for the most - *her man.* Her reoccurring concern is: "He doesn't understand my real need for pampering." Because women desire more feeling of security their pampered moments are the next best thing.

Women Are Making Positive Strides

Women have been changing for the past thirty years while men have looked on. They have changed how they think, work, have fun and how they take care of themselves. These changes are helping women make positive strides in their lives and part of this change has included their me-time moments.

Women are seeking and incorporating pampering treats in their lives and this book is full of many. Many women have been so career and goal oriented they've neglected to pamper themselves. Don't get me wrong, women are doing things to look sexier; like buying sexier clothes, reading sexier books, or buying sexier shoes, but that doesn't make them really feel pampered, they're simply more sexy … and there lies the problem.

After reading this book and putting these pampered tips into practice you will definitely experience more happiness and self-love. Most women who have read this book have already benefited from the ideas presented.

I offer this book, as a reminder of many things women should know. To help you improve your love life and enhance your sexuality, this book provides tips, treats and techniques that will definitely guide you toward a more pampered way of life.

Keep in mind that this is not a contest. It's about acquiring wisdom and knowledge on how to best pamper yourself. This is the key to being irresistible and living a good life, one that is full of joy and completeness from the inside out. Now, if you really want to learn more about pampering take this book, go to your special place and let's get started.

Who you are is your authentic self -- the self that God meant for you to be. Discovering what you know about yourself is the core of your emotional and spiritual self.

6

Creating A Place You Can Call Your Space

Your special space should be reserved for absorption, self-nurturing, reading, thinking and meditating uninterrupted.

Y ou've, no doubt, heard the phrase "Find a place to call your space." It's typically used when someone needs to "regroup", "calm down", or "unwind". It is important that you find a quiet place in your home to rest your mind. A place you can retreat to relax your body, refresh your spirit, and renew your mind. Somewhere you can shed the cares and stresses of the world *layer by layer*. I know this may sound all "odd", but isn't it time for you to indulge in the ideal of you, no matter how strange it sounds?

Women Seek Private Places and Spaces

Studies are showing that more women are seeking private places to relax. Guess what, one of the best ways to relax is to spend quiet time alone. Getting away from the human race can be personally stimulating and rewarding.

A woman can easily find time to escape without losing compassion for her family. Her *private time* has rich possibilities for inner peace and personal development. Setting aside time to listen to yourself enhances your ability to see the world more clearly.

Where Should Your Place of Serenity Be?

Every woman should construct a place in her home where she can go to regroup, rethink, revitalize or simply reenergize. It should be the perfect spot to read, listen to music, or relax as long as she doesn't focus on stressful subjects.

First, find a place in your home that you can delegate as your special space. It should be private with enough space to think or meditate uninterrupted. Someplace comfortable where you can sit or lie and grab all the "down time" you need.

Look around your home. Do you have a spare closet or quiet corner of a room; maybe in a bedroom or study? Some place where you won't be interrupted by a telephone ringing or computer announcing that you have a message? It may be your living room couch, a recliner in the den, your bed, a chair at your kitchen table (for those of us who get antsy if we're too far from the coffee maker), or a comfortable chair at your computer desk. Truth be told, you probably all ready have a "spot" - you just haven't looked at it in this way.

Your loved ones should understand that when you go to this special space, your desire is to spend some quiet time in solitude for a short time. This space should also encourage quality of life such as healthiness, wholesomeness, and self-absorption.

Spend Time Getting Your View Just Right

When you have your place picked out, don't EVER let any worries or negative thoughts intrude upon it. If you happen to be in your quiet place, and the burdens of the world overtake your mind, either quiet them or move to another spot. Just do not allow these thoughts into your quiet place. Don't let them crash your relaxation party! God knows they'll try.

If you have a comfortable chair, position it with the back of the chair to the middle of the room so that you can look out a window. Spend some time getting the view just right. You may have to trim the branches of a tree or plant a beautiful window box. Be sure the view is soothing and not distracting.

Decorate Your Special Space

Decorate your special space with favorite things that make you feel comfortable. Place a small table next to the comfortable chair, one that is just big enough for a book, a cup, and a lamp. Don't be tempted to put too many things on the table. You don't want anything to distract you! You can bring your favorite drink to your place of comfort if you wish. It doesn't need to have any alcohol content, just as long as it is refreshing and satisfying to you.

If you were really seeking peace of mind, you wouldn't think of settling in without a soft, fluffy throw over the back of the chair in case it gets chilly.

Getting Situated In Your Special Place

Anytime you find it necessary to slow down from a hectic day go to your special space. Here, you can read, think, rediscover, rejuvenate or simply be left alone. Close the door; turn off the TV, radio and ringer on the telephone. Put on some soothing instrumental music, and relax to your heart's content. And don't be surprised if you doze off!

Close your eyes and relax for a few minutes. Try to think of all the good things that have happened in your life and bring those good thoughts to your mind. After a few minutes of meditation, open your eyes. You should begin to feel a sense of focus. Now, try to find answers to any questions you might have. Do not allow distractions to interfere as you work to get the answers you are seeking.

If your concentration breaks and you aren't able to meditate, don't give up. Sometimes it takes a few tries. Your mind and body has to get accustomed to you slowing them down at will. Now, try again. Relax, close your eyes and meditate. You may quietly talk to God, recite affirmations or simply think of nothing as you clear your mind.

After a while, relax again, breathe slowly, and meditate with your eyes closed and mind seeking focus. If you are still finding it difficult to focus take a few deep breathes and exhale slowly. Now, relax your body and begin your goal of finding focus again. You'll be pleasantly surprised at how your mind, body, and soul understands what is going on in your life and how spending quiet time in your special place can bring you the needed focus and peace of mind.

You have to find places where you recognize yourself ~Ellaism

7

Strengthening Your Senses
Nothing's better on earth than a woman and her ability to sense things.

W hile sitting in the back yard of our Desoto property one evening, my husband leaned over and whispered in my ear, "Listen to that joyful noise!" I could hear nothing so I asked, "What am I supposed to be listening for." "The beauty of quiet," he replied. I looked toward the sky and listened. I could hear it.

Savor Silence

Most of us become so accustomed to the noise and sounds around us that until our attention is drawn to the beauty of silence we're not aware of how noise invades our space. Beyond that we get so use to the absence of silence that we become kind of uncomfortable when faced with it.

Silence eliminate our distractions, and compels us to be alone with ourselves. Have you ever thought it was too noisy to think? Silence has the gift of helping you discover the most profound and meaningful inner pleasures.

Try to remember the last time you had even 30 minutes of complete silence. We live in such a noisy world. We wake up to the noise of an alarm clock, our electrical coffee maker, electrical toothbrushes, hairdryers, morning news, morning traffic reports, children crying, husbands yelling, engines roaring, horns tooting, phones ringing, etc. It's enough to make you loose your mind. Even our weekends are filled with noises, lawnmowers, leave blowers, children playing and any other noise that you've become accustomed to hearing.

Create silence in your own world. Bask in the pleasure of silence. You notice how you'll eventually come to cherish this innocent pleasure.

Enjoy Listening

We all know that silence is great, and it's helpful to learn how to tune out the bothersome noises we don't want. Occasionally we become so use to certain noises that we no longer hear them. Of course, this is good if you live near a noisy factory. In other instances, we could refer to this as selective listening. We tune out what we can't control and deal with everything else. When we do this we lose our ability to really listen to one another, to our inner voice and to the sweet, soothing sounds all around us.

Stand still, close your eyes and notice the farthest and closest noises you can make out. Can you hear the wind chime on the back porch, the wooden screen door closing, the creaking of the rocking chair, or the popcorn popping in the microwave? Be more aware of your emotional reaction to them. Now you'll be able to hear the pleasurable noises over the noisy factory. They've been there all the time.

You may find the sounds of home comforting - the dog cooing for attention, the grandchildren laughing at one another, your husband flipping the channels on the TV, your son running up and down the stairs, cell phone ringing, the battery operated clock ticking loudly, music playing or the air conditioning blowing. When you need a hug or if you're feeling a little lonely, tired, frazzled, why not lift your mood and energize your spirit with a few wonderful sounds.

Pamper Your Soul with Silence

Even though good conversation is also stimulating, remaining quiet for short periods of time has proven to be great for positive thinking. Effectively incorporating solitude in your life helps you relish and value life. During your silent times when you don't speak, answer the telephone, read newspapers, watch television or listen to the radio, you can listen to your inner voice instead.

When you maintain silence for a day or a major part of the day, you're experiencing the phenomenon of solitude. Some of the best times to solve problems are during silent times. Asking pertinent questions during silent times gives clarity, which in turn gives answers. Women tend to appreciate the input they receive from their surroundings as they draw energy from being silent.

Traditions of silence are ancient, and full of spiritual enlightenment. Silence is known as the *holy uselessness,"* a cleansing of interfering vision. Even though silence is described as passive, absence of noise - many philosophers consider it active and complex.

Silence is the voice of the soul. When you're talking or preparing to talk, you are deaf to songs within. A calmer mind is reflected during silence. Creativity flourishes as it provides a chance to grow from thoughts within. Silence can also free negative energies.

Finding a time to experience solitude will help enhance your thoughts, ideas and creativity. Psychiatrist Anthony Storer, M.D., author of *Solitude: A Return to the Self*, explains how a woman wrote him to tell how she escaped to her bedroom each afternoon, not because she needed sleep, but because she had to be alert to the needs of others without regards to her own. She indulged in silent moments during these times.

Listening to yourself helps you realize how much you really do or don't know. It helps reduce the expenditure of excessive energy. Initiating silence can bring peak moments of awareness to your life.

Create an Environment of Tranquility

Silence has been smothered in today's busy and noisy world of information. Reviving the value of silence is now being done at retreats, and religious centers so that the mind can be nourished by tranquility. Silence releases the power to express your self. Women are seeking contemplation in our society, and finding out that they don't have to leave home to obtain its benefits is great. Creating an environment to succeed with silent commitment is necessary to capture its true benefits. Here are some basic silence guidelines to follow:

1. Have the people with whom you live to actively cooperate. Cooperation is crucial to your growth in silence. Silence can sometimes feel like rejection to your loved ones, so explain why silent times are so important to you. Use these times, as enclosed curtains for yourself instead of a door to shut out loved ones will help you create support that you need from your family.

2. Share your silence. Being quiet together can add new life to your relationship. It's okay to smile, touch and look into each other's eyes from time to time with nonverbal communication.

3. Bring your children into your circle of silence. Encourage them to bring silent times into their own lives. It helps them to value the ability to concentrate as well as make graceful exits from arguments. It enables them to release stress by learning to calm themselves.

4. Schedule silent times. Set aside time in your day for being completely silent. You can choose the time of day as well as the amount of time you'll use. You're making time for you so you can make the rules. Remember that once you make the rules it will be easier to stick to them.

5. Explain your silent times. It's your decision whether or not you explain your personal solitude. People are going to form their own opinions regardless of the true reason why, so why not be unavailable during these times. After all isn't that the purpose of silent times?

6. Make use of the tools available to you. When out in public, wearing headphones without playing anything keeps people

from distracting you or talking to you. Use your answering machine to intercept your telephone calls while integrating silent times at home. Silence is new to many women, so exploration is different.

Other Ways to Spend Time During Solitude

The wonderful impacts that solitude is having on my life are beneficial in the ways that I spend my days. It helps to awaken my consciousness and strengthens my senses to the natural world around me.

When a bird chirps or the wind whistles I notice. I realized that I don't have to be active all the time, because I am content with being quietly me. Short sessions of solitude are appreciated because stillness is now a valuable opportunity to cherish me. I value and cherish times that I can be at peace with myself. Capturing the world of silence is an intimate relationship with ones-self.

You may want to do something different each time you reward your self with silence. You may choose to quietly cook, clean, garden, write poems or short stories. A quiet place offers creativity. Doing nothing at all is also nice for nourishing your soul. Why not try a few from this list just to get you going.

- ❖ Enjoy a long quiet ride alone in your car.
- ❖ Take a walk in the early morning dawn.
- ❖ Take a walk in the quiet evening dusk.
- ❖ Take a quiet walk along the beach.
- ❖ Suggest a silent bike ride with your lover.
- ❖ Encourage a quiet hike.

- ❖ Sit on top of a hill to recapture the essence of nature.
- ❖ Enclose yourself in your favorite room and lavish solitude upon yourself.

Delight In Touching

Touch has a profound effect on our sensibilities and our lives. We find comfort in the smallest things if we are allowed to indulge in our pleasurable moments. Still, we often miss the essential life elements and source of our real joy.

There have been many times - for no reason at all I massaged moisturizing gel on my husband's feet. He always seems pleasantly surprised. I guess the fact of the matter is he doesn't have to ask for it, I offer it gladly when I feel that he needs a gentle touch. This simple act of touching brings us closer.

As a young girl I remember stroking my puppy and that always made me feel good, but he would lie flat as a rug and welcome my touch. I would always wonder how good that would feel to have my parents stroke my tummy from time to time. I suppose it just looked like it felt good. As I got grown, I loved when my children would play in my hair or brushed it. That felt so good to me. Even small gestures as regular as walking hand in hand with my 22 year-old son makes me feel proud. It always brings a smile to my face when he grabs my hand as if he helping me do something. I see it as the protective order of things. That feels good too.

When I see those bumper stickers that say... "Hug your child!" or 'When was the last time you were given a hug." They are both special reminders that the magic of touch is really a gift from God.

Use Scents That Soothe

Fresh flowers scattered about your home, clean bed linens, fresh smelling clothing, clean smelling home and baked cookies fill the air. Fresh cut grass, turkey roasting in the oven and clothes drying in the dryer brings back memories of care-free days. These are all familiar scents that soothe the mind and help me recall memories of the way things use to be. What are your memories?

I remember spending long hours in the kitchen watching my Aunt Lela cook pastries. She was the family baker. Every Sunday Aunt Lela would cook enough cakes and pies to share with three generations of cousins, aunts, uncles and grandparents. At home, everyday I would wake up to the smell of hot tea, toast, eggs and bacon. I especially remember the smell of homemade buttered biscuits.

Anytime I choose, I can close my eyes and be instantly transported back to a more carefree place and time. In other memories I am surrounded by the comforting scents of my grandmothers house; the homemade baseball bases in my backyard, the huge homemade flowerbed that the whole family chipped in to build, the attic with no windows and Mt Zion Baptist church I attended every Sunday. Each one of these places had their own special scent too. It makes me wish I could turn back the hands of time!

According to scientists, aromas directly affect the brain. The sense of smell is 100 times more potent than any of our other senses. Maybe it's because our brain registers aromas twice as fast as it does pain.

To benefit from the restorative comfort and healing properties of fragrance, try sprinkling your favorite scented oil on a handkerchief.

Sniff it when you need to relax and watch the properties of the oils go to work.

Noise and Its Stressful Effects

For women, it's a well know fact that the stress of noise and the rigors of daily life can affect the way you look. The simple solution is used to pamper yourself whenever you can.

For decades women have worked hard at keeping their exteriors beautiful. They have religiously exfoliated, cleansed, toned and moisturized their skin, but according to the latest beauty gurus, beauty really does come from within.

For some time now, the New-Age jargon has taught us that looking good comes from feeling good about oneself. If a woman feels healthy and happy, her skin has a better chance of glowing. Which is why, these days, hands-on beauty treatments are designed to pamper the person as well as her skin. As a result, at least 50% of a treatment's effectiveness is down to the relaxation, not just creams on the skin.

This holistic view of beauty will make sense to anyone who has experienced a stress-induced skin outbreak or a period of dull hair, dull skin and broken nails after an illness.

No matter how much concealer and make-up we use, we really only look our best when we feel our best - and this is more than just a psychological phenomena, it has it's basis in physiological reality.

A relaxed person actually has increased superficial circulation and more of the hormones, which control healing, and cell replication, as well as more of the endorphins, which give us the feel good factor.

When we are stressed, it does cause beauty problems because of the physiological changes it causes in our bodies. When we're under pressure, our muscles tighten and restrict the blood flow to every part of our body.

At the same time, it slows down the lymphatic drainage into and out of every organ so that the cells cannot defend themselves from infection. Indigestion, constipation, irritable bowel syndrome and bloating can all be a result and, at the same time, you might notice that you have dull, shallow skin that is prone to spots, strange bumps, allergic reactions and chapped lips that are prone to sores.

When you consider that the skin is the largest organ of the body, and that it also feeds the hair and nails, it's not surprising that stress quickly manifests itself in the way we look.

Of course, the difficulty with stress-related beauty problems is that it's rather difficult to eliminate the cause. Stress is part and parcel of most of our lives, and the secret is learning how to cope with it. If the thought of traditional stress management techniques leaves you cold, it's worthwhile remembering that some of the best ways to relax also involve some of the best beauty treatments.

A new generation of pampering treats work on you from the outside. For example... A facial will deep-cleanse your complexion and will also soothe and relax your mind, while aromatherapy oils, which moisturize your skin, will ease tense muscles and boost your energy level.

Most beauty and health spas today follow one principle: Relax the person and they will automatically look and feel better!

Holistic beauty therapies these days cleverly use complementary treatments to leave us pampered, refreshed and revived.

Aromatherapy started the trend when it was discovered that essential oils worked on the skin and the mind, but other complementary therapies have followed suit, including reflexology, shiatsu massage and acupressure.

What was traditionally the domain of the alternative therapist is now a part of the beautician's portfolio and I don't hear anyone complaining.

Recite affirmations, prayers or reminders while showering. Imagine your showers as showers of blessings.

8

Stock Your Pampering Pantry

*There are few hours in life more agreeable than the hour or so
dedicated to pampering rituals.*

W omen often have what they refer to as their pampering pantry, or goodie drawer. This is the place a woman can safely store and preserve her pampering supplies.

Your pampering pantry doesn't have to take up a whole cabinet, simply clear a shelf or two in your closet or cabinet and stock it with essentials. You can even store your supplies in a pretty basket under the counter or sink. As with any pampering pantry you will need a few basics, plus some of your favorite ingredients to spice things up. With the right products and tools on hand, your pampering experience becomes a pleasure.

Pampering Products and Tools

Many pampering treatments include cleansing and moisturizing your skin, so keep on hand a few shower gels and body lotions you enjoy, scented with both invigorating and relaxing aromas. Another must have is a good neutral base oil such as jojoba or almond, which you can blend with essential oils for aromatherapy treatments and massages. (There are also many preblended oils you might like, which take away the guesswork of mixing your own.) To stock your essential oils collection, begin with a few whose scent and effects appeal to you, and build from there. Pampering Pleasures suggests many specific oils and describes their benefits in later sections.

Scrubs, Polishes and Glows

You'll want to have a salt and a sugar scrub as basic staples. Each of these products exfoliates the skin. Bath salts, a good body mud, and facemasks are other basics that are considered beneficial treats.

High quality face, body and hair care products such as antioxidants, moisturizers, body buffers, replenishing shampoos and conditioners are also great to include in your pampering props and supplies inventory.

The best pampering tools are plain and simple. One of the most essential is the humble loofah. The great natural sponge is available whole (it looks like a cylinder) or made into mitts. Either way, it works wonders for helping improve circulation and exfoliating skin. Brushes come in all shapes and sizes; you'll need a large one for your body and a small complexion brush for your face, plus a good quality hairbrush.

Other basic tools include emery boards, orange sticks, cotton balls, a nail buffer, a pumice stone, and a foot file. For extra pampering, include hand mitts and foot booties for deep overnight skin hydration.

Use neck pillows, eye pillows and massage tools for soothing and relaxing your muscles.

Comforting Touches

A pampering experience wouldn't be complete without some special touches that add more comfort. First make sure the space you're using is tidy - rumpled laundry and linens and leftover bath toys can spoil the mood. Put them away and in their proper places.

Have clean fluffy towels and a thick robe available. Try indulging yourself with chenille blankets and soft flannel sheets washed in lavender to bring home the feelings of a luxurious pampering experience.

Aromatherapy diffusers and candles add both the beauty of low light and the benefits of scent to your spa experience.

Every woman should have at least one place of enchantment to turn to.

9

Essential Oils That Pamper, Heal and Relax

This chapter will provide an entrancing introduction to the gentle art of aromatherapy and a fascinating look at the most popular essential oils.

There are a few simple luxuries that are as pleasing as soaking in a fragrant bath or being massaged with aromatic oils. There are only a few healing arts as enjoyable as aromatherapy baths and even fewer tonics as enticing as the pure plant essences known as essential oils.

Since ancient times, essential oils have been thought to benefit the body, mind and emotions. Different oils can be used to treat and prevent all manner of health problems, and they are widely used to relax, rejuvenate, soothe or stimulate. Oils encourage wonderful feelings of well-being and women who use them create wonderful moods of indulgence for their senses.

Since ancient times essential oils have been thought to benefit the body, mind, and spirit. Historical manuscripts tell of fragrances from plants as ingredients in charms and ceremonies, as well as in remedies, cosmetics, and food.

In the Middle Ages, Monks cultivated herbs and discovered many of their restorative properties. They were among the first to distil precious plant essences, carefully blending them into liquors to be administered to patients. These concentrated pure plant extracts revered for their fragrance and their therapeutic value, is termed as essential oils. The use of such oils is known as aromatherapy.

Many essential oils are believed to have special properties, ranging from antiseptic to aphrodisiac in effect. Some promote relaxation and a generally good feeling. Others stimulate and rejuvenate. All encourage a feeling of well-being and can be used to treat or prevent health problems, or they can be used to create a mood and pamper your senses.

Chamomile is useful for tension and insomnia; rosemary is good for poor circulation and fatigue, peppermint is a tried and true remedy for indigestion, common sage can prevent muscular problems and sandalwood has a relaxing and tonifying effect on the nervous system.

There are many ways to experience the benefits from essential oils, which involve either breathing in the enticing aromas or absorbing the diluted oils through the skin. Because essential oils are highly concentrated, it is not usually advisable to apply them directly to the skin or to ingest them, unless advised by a skilled therapist.

Aromatherapy Oils

Essential oils penetrate the skin very quickly to reach the bloodstream and are therefore a marvelous accessory to massage therapy. The concentrated oil should be added to a much greater quantity of oil known as 'carrier' or 'base' oil. These should have a neutral odor and be easily absorbed. Light vegetable or nut oils such as almond, apricot kernel, grapeseed, soya, and peach kernel are popular choices.

Massage Oils

Good ones do not absorb into the skin too quickly so they last longer while you're softly kneading away. You should also be very conscientious of the scents that you select. Heavenly scented oils have a tendency to be overwhelming.

Massage oil tips that help you choose what's best for you.

1. Aromatherapy is a wonderful way to select which scents you and your partner would like since certain scents produce specific effects. Lavender, for instance, puts people to sleep, while eucalyptus wakes people up, but it may be too powerful for sensitive skin.

2. Wherever you shop for it, consult the clerks because they will know what works best for you.

3. Do not make up too much massage oil at one time as the fragrance spoils after a short while.

4. A few drops of your selected essential oil in three tablespoons of carrier oil should be sufficient for a nice massage.

5. Adding wheatgerm oil or vitamin E to your mixture can help to prevent it from turning rancid.

6. Storing your massage oils in a corked bottle should be sufficient or a flip top plastic bottle. The latter is most convenient because it is less likely to spill if toppled.

7. Dark bottles are best because they help reduce discoloration and deterioration of essential oils in any form.

Inhalants or Room Fresheners

The various essential oils have different influences on our mood. To use them as an inhalant or as a room freshener, try experimenting with the following combinations.

1. To stimulate the mind try rosemary, sage or thyme

2. To create a feminine aura try rose, geranium, or jasmine

3. To compliment a celebration, use; rose or jasmine

4. To clear the mind try lavender, sandalwood, or lemongrass

5. For a healing atmosphere in a sick room; rose, bay, or thyme

6. For meditation choose lavender, ylang-ylang, or jasmine.

Inhalation may be used to relieve headaches and clear congestion that accompanies colds or sinusitis. To make a simple steam inhalation, add two to four drops of your selected essential oil - eucalyptus, thyme, and tea tree are recommended - to a bowl of very hot water. Lean over it, tent your head with a towel, and breathe in the vapor for at least three to five minutes.

To disseminate essential oils in wider environments clay or ceramic vaporizers can be used to heat water or can be kept near the oils. Electric vaporizers or light bulbs are also great options. There are hollow clay rings that contain essential oil and can be slipped over light bulbs so that the room is filled with fragrance once the bulb heats up. Simplest of all these methods are the plastic pump spray bottle; just fill with warm water and your favorite essential oil. Shake and use to mist a room and enliven it with fresh scent.

The fragrance of essential oils can be enjoyed without any extra equipment. Soak a cotton ball in essential oil and place either in a room or in a cupboard to scent the area. For a fuller effect, place somewhere warm, such as behind a heater or fireplace. Sprinkle logs or twigs with lavender oil before placing then on the fire, or use rosemary on the wood for a fabulous permeating aroma. If you have a congested nose, a single drop of suitable oil, such as cypress or eucalyptus, on a tissue or handkerchief can offer wonderful relief.

Aromatherapy Baths

An important part of aromatherapy is aromatic baths, which can be detoxifying, relaxing, or reviving, depending on the oil(s) you choose. They are wonderful just before bed, both to help reduce pain or to dispel stress which may keep you awake.

To prepare an aromatherapy bath, simply add two drops of your favorite selected oils, to a warm bath, stir to ensure the oil is evenly dispersed, and then relax in the scented water. A ten-minute soak should give the desired effect. Variations on aromatic bathing include a sitz or hipbath, or footbaths. Essential oils may also be used in the shower and on compresses to ease muscular aches, sprains and bruises.

10

Illumination & Lighting

*In this chapter you will understand how illumination establishes a
sense of energy, serenity and a mood for pampering.*

P ampering spaces requires careful attention. A pampering area needs plenty of ambient or general illumination as well as task lights dedicated to each station of pampering space. If you take time to plan it to fit your moods you should be fine with what you end up with. Your lighting is a reflection of what you like, want and need so do it like you want it done. The main thing you'll have to remember is your room's lighting must be subtle and stirring, functional and atmospheric. It must be adjustable to meet the demands of day and night or to vary the mood of the space. Well-planned lightning can meet all of these needs.

Planning Your Lighting

Before you plan your lighting think about the space you are placing the lighting. Bathrooms and bedroom lighting are different. You would not want to rely on natural light in a bathroom, but it would add lots of ambience to a bedroom. Your pampering pleasure lighting plan begins at your focal point and moves from there.

Surround mirrors with clear soft lighting to avoid shadows and glare on your face. Scones and strip lights are great for this. In the shower where space is often enclosed and limited lighting should be bright enough to shave during day or night hours.

Bathtubs need good lighting. Try a recessed fixture or a can light, and direct the beam outside the tub to prevent bounce back off the water.

If you really want lighting that makes you feel totally pampered seek fixtures with translucent glass shades, because they reduce glare significantly and can help create a diffused glow. Pay attention to the direction that your fixtures aim their light: scones can cast light in different directions, including up, down and sideways. For a nice ambient radiance, think about indirect lighting, which usually recesses the light source in an overhead cove (hence the term 'cove lighting').

It's important to understand what qualities of light will work best for pampering times, both with your skin tone and the materials in the bath. The goal is to provide the room with a background of flattering, even light. If your bath has lots of high gloss figures or surfaces, use low-wattage lighting on the walls and ceiling to help avoid glare and to create a soft glow. Think of how wonderful you will feel after pampering yourself. Getting out of the tub in the most flattering light and seeing yourself will enhance your inner spirit

To change the mood of installed lighting in the bath or to add a decorative flourish, use accent lighting. Floor lamps, table lamps, or chandeliers can all function as accent lights. To further change the mood of bathroom lighting, install dimmer switches. Nightlights can provide a needed beacon in a dark house or illumination for a midnight pampering moments.

Create a Room for Reflection

Light is both a great wave and a tiny particle. Take inspiration from the wonders of physics to design personal lighting plan for your bath. Use natural light by day and make it a romantic retreat at night using spots and sparkles of candlelight and crystal.

Be bold. Be flexible. The more types of lighting you use and the variety of fixtures, the greater your ability to adapt the ambience to suit your mood. Dress up your bath for the evening with candles (more on candles later in this chapter) and accessorize that sparkle and shine. Dress it down in the daytime with draperies that allow lots of natural light to shine through. Add reflective accents so that light dances from surface to surface. Maybe your bath could incorporate suspended fixtures hung with beads and crystals, and uses silver accessories to establish a mood more alluring than the traditional bathroom.

Lights and candles are tools that help you shape your space. Different intensities and wide to narrow light beams can highlight distinct areas within a larger environment; different wall colors can make the light in a space seem brighter. A lush jewel tone like matte, sapphire, blue, or cobalt blue absorbs light and remains a vivid backdrop, even in full sun. At night, candles and chandeliers describe their own magical circles, creating soothing pools of light around a room.

Does your bath have large or numerous windows that flood the interiors with lots of daylight? Is your bathroom generous with dramatic or romantic lighting? Do have intriguing light fixtures that draw attention and create luminous points of interests? All of these things give your bathroom space more presence. Take a look around your bath and imagine the possibilities.

Light is a natural luxury. Capture its flickering radiance with mirrors, glass and other silvery surfaces. Find bulbs that approximate the intensity and color of light at your favorite time of day, and then use them with dimmers so that you can increase or decrease the level of light. Experiment by using bulbs of different wattages to create lighting contrast. Lower-watt bulbs produce a softer cast of light than brighter high-wattage bulbs.

Light Fixture Tricks

Be creative with light fixtures. Just by changing the number of watts, the color or the wash of light in a bathroom you can create a variety of moods. Try different lamp shades for different qualities of light; colored silk softens and tints light; paper and linen provide a gentle milky glow. Create a radiant atmosphere around the bath with candlelight hung low overhead and mixed with fairy lights at one side. Candelabra on the floor, below the level of your face will cast light upward for a glamorous effect. And don't forget candles.

Remember to use Candles

Harness the positive energy of candles. Candles should adorn every woman's home. They are great addition to your pampering rituals. Bring in pillars, votives, and scented candles to create a true sense of private refuge. As you read this book or have *'me time'* light a candle. Say aloud or in your mind any affirmations or prayers, and think positive thoughts. Make a commitment to yourself to improve your life by raising your level of spiritual consciousness.

An indulgent way to spend an evening alone is to turn your own bedroom into a candlelit palace. Do this just for yourself. Place scented candles all about your room, group them in strategic corners and places and create a glamorous and cozy boudoir to sit and read while in bed. Reading in bed undisturbed is truly one of a woman's greatest luxuries. Try reading other books on pampering and luxury. Read books that give you a peak into the world of luxury and prestige. A lazy evening reading by candlelight can easily create a sense of feeling luxurious.

No matter what it is you want to accomplish - better health, to finding a new career, connecting with loved ones, or protection and happiness for your family - use your candles to help you get in your pampering zone. Your candles will help light the way to peace, serenity and relaxation for a renewed inner and outer self.

Assign a Message to Your Candles

Light your candles, then assign a message to each. Relax and surround yourself with the flicker of pampering candles. Light your candles and imagine your lifestyle once you've achieved all your personal goals. As you visualize your goals think of how you're going to achieve them down to the tiniest detail. Be specific. Program your mind for success. See yourself achieving your goals.

Ask yourself. What do I want out of life? Healing, financial success, spiritual awareness, better health, start a family, new career, love, new house, protection, longevity, guidance peace. Focus on one goal at a time. Light a candle for each, and then do one thing every day that will help achieve your dreams.

What Candle Colors Represent

White candle for peace on earth.

Jasmine candle to raise your spiritual consciousness.

Red candle for strength and good health.

Light blue candle for healing, understanding and harmony.

Dark blue candle for inspiration, protection and meditation.

Green candle for money, growth, prosperity and abundance.

Yellow candle for confidence, action.

Brown candle for endurance and concentration.

Pink candle for love, honor and affection.

Orange candle for stimulation.

Purple candle for communication.

Gold candle for physical strength, knowledge and wisdom.

Silver candle for stability.

Violet candle for self-improvement.

Black candle for truth and releasing painful memories.

Lavender candle for blessings.

Romance:

Light floating candles and burn your favorite scented candles to create a romantic atmosphere.

Family:

Arrange your candles in groupings that represent and symbolize members of your family. Combine small, medium and tall candles to serve as the family unit. As you light your candles recite a prayer for each family member. Take this image and surround your family in this protective bubble. Ask God to keep your loved ones safe.

Candles in a cluster are a great way to symbolize your friends and loved ones - giving out light to all who see and feel their energy. It is believed that tall candles reaching to the sky are messages to God. Each time you light a candle with love in your heart you increase your awareness of how to heal from the inside out. It's a universal truth that candles represent unity, peace, love and spirituality.

A Little Candle History

Early candles were made of vegetable waxes produced from plants such as bayberries, candelilla leaves, candle tree bark, esparto grass, and various varieties of palm leaves such as carnuba and ouricury. They were also made of animal tissue and secretions, such as spermaceti (whale oil), ambergris, and beeswax (insect secretions).

Sometimes entire animals such as the stormy petrel and the candlefish of the Pacific Northwest were threaded with a wick and burned as candles. Tallow candles were made of sheep, cow, or pig fat.

All these candles were rather crude, time-consuming to make and very smoky.

Kinds of Candles FYI

Of the two kinds of candle fuel, beeswax was considered the better since it burned cleaner than tallow and had a lovely odor compared to tallow's rancid, smoky smell. Being scarce, beeswax was expensive. Only churches and the wealthy could afford beeswax candles. By the 17th century, European state edicts controlled the weight, size and cost of candles. In 1709, an act of the English Parliament banned the making of candles at home unless a license was purchased and a tax paid.

Probably most important of all, Paraffin was refined from oil around 1850, making petroleum-based candles possible. The combination of paraffin, which burns clean and without odor; and stearins, which harden soft paraffin, was developed in the nineteenth century. It revolutionized the candle industry, giving us the tools and materials we still use for candle manufacturing.

Understanding Candle Shapes

Container: Any candle that is poured into a container and burned in the container is a container candle. These candles are made of soft wax and would not be able to stand on their own outside their enclosures. The container prevents soft wax from dripping. These candles are safely contained in a vessel, and used in restaurants and religious rituals that require long-burning candles.

Pillar: A thick candle with geometrical cross section such as a circle, oval, or hexagon is called a pillar. It is referred to by its diameter followed by its height. For example, a 3-by 6-inch pillar would be 3 inches in diameter and 6 inches high. Pillars come in standard sized for commercial and religious purposes.

Novelty: These are irregularly shaped candles made by molding, sculpting and/or pouring.

Taper: These are long cylindrical candles that kindle memories of historic candle-dipping. Tapers are generally 1/2 inch or 7/8 inch in diameter at the base because most holders are designed to fit these two sizes. There are, of course, exceptions, such as birthday candles (3/16 inch) and Danish tapers (1/4 inch).

Votive and Tea Lights: Although these candles originated in the church, the term now refers to small plug-type candles that are 1 1/2 inches in diameter by 2 to 3 inches high. This shape has become popular for scented candles because their small size allows them to fit easily into small rooms, such as bathrooms.

As votives melt and become liquid in their containers, the wick uses up all the liquid fuel. If you burn a votive on a plate, the burn time will be shorter because the wax will drip and the wick will be unable to use it. Tea lights are small votives used to warm pots of potpourri and to heat foods. They fit in smaller-than-standard votive cups.

11

Enjoy In-Home Massages

Enjoy luxurious treatments in the comfort and convenience of your home with the same details that you experience in a spa.

E veryone likes to be touched in *that* special kind of way. And although we love massages, they are a thousand times more enjoyable when done by a sexy lover. Massages can be used for anything from calming your nerves from a tough day at work to getting primed for a relaxing evening with your partner.

To prepare for this wonderful in-home excursion, you'll need a few mood setters and techniques. Below are some suggestions that will help spruce up your nights of rubdown heaven.

Set the Environment

Close the lights and ignite lots of same-scent candles. Again, aromatherapy can be a big payoff, but select something that is lightly scented and neutral. If you like, you can even burn some incense to create a more relaxing environment.

Getting Ready

Wrap yourself in a towel. Warm some oil in your hands and work the tendons at the back of the neck with your fingertips. Gently rub the arms and shoulders. Rub the temples slowly in circular motions and massage the jaw area since it usually contains a lot of tension.

Try rubbing yourself first. Rub your shoulders, hands, wrist, knees, legs, ankles, etc. It will make you feel more in the mood. It will also help you prep your hands for your partner.

Do's and Don'ts

Before getting started read this section to your partner. It will help inform him of the do and don'ts of administering a pampering massage.

After reading this section together lye in the nude (or semi-nude) with your stomach down on the bed and make sure you're in a comfortable position. Smooth the oil over the entire back in wide, smooth strokes with the flat part of the palm. Try not to knead the body too intensely because it may end up causing more pain than comfort.

Rub slowly and deeply, remembering to be continuously sensual. Devote all the time in the world to the person you are massaging. Make it very personal. Reach out to him and assure him that he can touch you whenever he wants.

When massaging, work your way down from the back of the neck to the shoulders. Don't squeeze too hard around the neck area because you may end up causing an unwanted choking sensation. If you're working the shoulders, be careful not to squeeze the collarbones with the muscle because it's an agonizing sensation.

Stretch out the arms and massage the biceps lightly with your fingertips. Work the back on either side of the spinal cord, but never push deeply on the spine itself. Use upward strokes laterally along the spine until you reach the tailbone. Feel free to tease the area around the base of the spine because it contains many sensitive nerve endings.

Rubbing the Right Way

While you're rubbing, lean over and let your chest rub against his back ever so slightly. Let other parts of your body rub against him while in the midst of your massage. From time to time exhale slowly and when you're about to end the session, nibble on the ear. By the time you're done rubbing the body down, there will be much more than just rubbing on the mind.

After you've done the back and arms, work your way down to the legs, especially the inner thighs because they are incredibly sensitive. The legs should be given special care. You don't have to be as cautious as with the back, but still remain gentle. Rub the legs one section at a time, starting at the thighs, moving to the calves and finally ending at the feet. Don't stay on the feet too long or it will cause sleepiness.

Massages are used for anything from calming after a tough day at work to getting primed for some enthusiastic lovemaking.

12

Restorative Rituals for Your Mind, Body, and Soul

*Every woman's should be able to look at her body and say with confidence…
"I've fallen in love with you."*

A re your days filled with agendas and meeting deadlines, counting calories, eating more fiber, taking vitamins, keeping up with the children, carpool, car repairs and practical self-love? Would you rather enjoy the simple pleasures of life? Every since I started writing about living your life to the fullest, I've seen a mad dash for simple things in life that bring pleasure. People, women in general want to revive their minds, bodies and souls.

These restorative 'me-time rituals' are easy to implement. They enhance a woman's creative nature and heal areas of her life that are out of balance. Most women take life serious and work so hard to achieve goals and acquire things; that they often forget about the simple joys that enrich their souls. We question anything that we gain ordinary pleasure from. We question our own attempt to find love, peace and happiness so to speak. We have become so uninspired by life that we question anything or anybody that helps us get inspired about the small things that could make us happy. We have been so conditioned to work hard for our happiness that we deprive ourselves of playful spontaneity. Today we stop depriving and began enriching. Let's began with restorative rituals.

Phase 1: Improve Your Touch

Let's begin by doing something very simple. Go to the secluded spot of your choice...it can be your special place, your lounge, or your bed. This skill will test your memory skills.

What you'll need: a secluded space, different sized and different shaped hard objects of your choice.

Close your eyes and let your body go limp. Bring the different objects to your secluded place. Examples are: balls, fruit, cucumbers, carrots, bottles, soaps, and sponges.

Memorize these objects. Recall their size, shape, length, width and texture. Think of each and compare their differences. What are your likes and dislikes about these objects. You'll be amazed and excited about how good your memory is.

For a week, practice on your memory skills to increase your awareness of shapes, sizes and textures. This also improves your ability to touch your partner in sensitive and more caring ways. You can change out the items each day and discover how they come to life in your hands as you touch, feel, and caress them.

Now, close your eyes and bring out your sensitive side with each touch. Get mentally lost in how each object feels. Notice their shapes, size, textures, grooves, etc. This will help you become better at visualizing things by touch, texture and size.

Phase 2: Awaken Your Senses

In this ritual you'll use your mind to arouse your appetite and you'll begin to feel more sensually awakened. If you practiced Phase One as suggested, you should be able to move into this phase with ease.

What you'll need: your mind, your body and your favorite lotion.

To help improve your senses, massage your favorite lotion onto your body with your eyes closed. Use the following exercises as a way to find mental pleasure in the smallest thing you do. These exercises are designed to help you coast into the pleasure center of your brain. Imagine ...

❖ Slowly moisturizing your body while blindfolded. Moisturize every part of your body that you can reach. Don't be shy or inhibited. Once you imagine the eroticism of it, you'll be able to feel the pleasure of it.

❖ Massage your scalp or shampoo it in the shower with your eyes closed. Allow your happy feelings to kick in while you wash. Enjoy and love how you touch your own scalp.

- ❖ Take a bath with your partner sometimes. While doing so wrestle naked playfully. Continue the fun after stepping out of the tub or shower.
- ❖ Putting on some mellow music and dance slowly. Dance to the beat of the background music. Really feel your body move and understand how you are in control of each movement you make. Feel good and let your body continue to feel good too.
- ❖ Taking a shower in a darkened room with a small tea light candle. Enjoy the sensuality of your body and feel the presence of you in your own world… enjoying your moments.
- ❖ Wear a pair of satin boxers and notice how they feel against your body.
- ❖ Reading *Pampering Pleasures* to your lover - as erotically as you can.
- ❖ Giving and getting wonderful foot massages, and relaxing back rubs.
- ❖ Kissing your lover passionately every time you kiss.
- ❖ Giving full hugs every time you embrace your lover.

Ummmmm, imagine these wonderful pleasures as you learn how to awaken your senses.

Phase 3: Indulge In Baths (Stimulate)

In a woman's world of hectic schedules she'll do good to enjoy a bath for fifteen minutes, but it would be quite difficult for her to bath daily for five to six hours at a time. Be assured that a fifteen to twenty minute bath at least once a week can do wonders for any desiring woman. Baths pamper your outer and inner self.

Here's how you can enhance any bathing techniques you learn.

1. Pick the best time for bathing. Make sure you are free from any interruptions.

2. Lay out what you need for a comforting bath. Towels, loofah, candles, robe, scents, pillow, music, etc.

3. Shower first. Open your pores by showering first. Use long handled loofah for scrubbing and circulation.

4. Add your favorite scents. Perfumes or favorite body sprays add a sense of allure and sensuality to your bath.

5. Try different kinds of baths on each bathing occasion. Try bubbles one week, then maybe milk or champagne to your next bath. Try using flowers, colorful bath gels etc. You can consult with the experts in bath stores to get other great ideas and great products.

6. Soak. Soaking relieves tired muscles, soothes joints, and helps rid your body of minor aches and pains.

7. Listen to your favorite sounds. Play your favorite music, read or simply relax on your favorite bath pillow.

8. Cleanse your face. Apply your favorite masque or cream. They really work well with steam and help open pores.

9. Scrub, brush and loofah. After you've soaked for a while, scrub away dead skin with a nice bath brush or loofah. Manicure your cuticles while soaking and they become less bothersome.

10. Dry with e rubbing. Rubbing promotes circulation so rub your skin briskly, not hard with a wash a terry washcloth.

11. Complete your bath by applying your favorite body scent. Apply your favorite cologne or powder after your bath. Don't overdo it.

Use bathing to jump-start your pampering pleasures. Enjoy them, become a part of them, grow with them and shine because of them.

Jump Start Romance with Soothing Baths

Any bath can be used as a means of sensual stimulation toward other fulfilling moments. Your mind, body and love life will benefit from these baths.

What you'll need: Steam, water, scents and ability to touch.
The most important element of a sensually pampered bath experience is the ability to indulge and the time to do it. It's been the same since people flocked to public steam baths in ancient Sparta. While bathing and pampering helps women care for their bodies; the rituals of bath treatments help unify mind, body and spirit for overall well-being. (Also see types of spas)

Spas have been built for the same reasons, but their design and features continue to change. The palatial ancient Roman baths of Carcalla, Diocletian were set in huge gardens and included swimming pools, sporting areas, galleries, and libraries.

Russian banyas feature steam baths, cold pools and platzas (which consist of whacking the skin with soaking oak branches). Women all over the world have used sweat lodges both to purify the body and spirit and to communicate with their ancestors. Japanese sentos (penny baths) typically have both hot and cold pools and traditionally offer shiatsu massage.

Today bathing therapy increasingly addresses our more active and inquisitive lifestyles. Bathing is so popular because it restores the body, balances life, revives the mind and energizes the spirit.

Phase 4: Moisturize: Train Your Body

Body treatments are offered everywhere, from chair massages in grocery stores to full-day pampering at luxury spas. You should do a moisturizer treat each night before falling asleep. Start by telling everyone that you would like some privacy and relaxation, then go to your room and start your body therapy.

What you'll need: Music, moisturizer, scented candle, bathtub, and a fluffy bath towel.

- ❖ **Run a warm bath and add a spritz** of your favorite bath oil, cologne, or fragrance. While your water is filling in the tub, rub your body down with your favorite before-bath moisturizer and scan *Pampering Pleasures.*

- ❖ **Play your favorite music.** Next, unwind and let your senses lock in.

- ❖ **Light a small scented candle,** turn the lights off and ease into your freshly filled tub of water. Allow the water to envelope your awaiting body. Relax completely; this includes physically and mentally. Let the light from the candle dance in your mind as it flickers you into an intensely mellow mood.

❖ **Guide your mood toward relaxation**. Enhance your senses as you think of nothing but relaxation and sensual pleasures. Allow your quiet surroundings to swallow you up as the scents entice you. Let the mood romance your desires as you humble your soul to the pleasures of it all.

❖ **Now, pull a hand full of water** toward you and feel the water as it trickles down your chest, between your breast and across your neck. Ummmm that should feel soooo good.

❖ **Close your eyes now and listen to the music** playing softly as you gather your senses and adore the peacefulness that surrounds you. Discover the smoothness of the water as the ripples of water disappear. Get lost in your thoughts and when you begin to feel drowsy, remove your new self from your tub. Pat yourself dry with a fluffy towel, lightly moisturize again, get in bed and drift off to sleep.

Phase 5: Become Friends with Your Body

In this phase you will learn how to enjoy your own body. Each person's body is unique, and no matter what kind of body you have you are very special. Enjoy yourself as you discover you. Have pride in you, and your body. You will experience what makes you feel pampered.

What you'll need: bath towel, scented candles, lotion or moisturizer,

❖ After a soothing bath take your towel and dry off very slowly. With every stroke of your towel blot yourself gently as if you are drying off a newborn baby.

- ❖ Slowly massage your body with your favorite lotion, oil or moisturizer - trying not to miss any areas.

- ❖ Applying by candlelight is very soothing and spiritual. Begin a friendship with your body. Know where every hump, bump and mole is on your body. Get to know your body! Once you've rubbed on any remaining lotion, pull your bed covers back and ease into your bed while naked.

- ❖ *Pampered* is how you should feel. For a moment, think only good thoughts about the skin you are in. Enjoy the body you have been blessed with. In a short while you should fall asleep. Sweet dreams. Don't forget to blow out candles.

Phase 6: Energize Your Body

Instead of hitting the snooze button, chugging caffeine and gulping breakfast, try easing into your day by adding one or several spa treatments to your morning ritual. A few minutes of simple self-care can help you enjoy the start of each new day, one invigorating step at a time.

What you'll need: bath brush, sisal washcloth or wash mitt, scented gel, and towel.

- ❖ **Dry Brushing:** Dry brushing your skin is great for circulation. It helps oxygenate cells and carry impurities away through the lymph system. You should begin with your back using light pressure and lightly brushing your arms and legs, using an upward motion. Brush toward your chest to move fluids and circulation toward your heart.

73

❖ **Exfoliating Scrub:** Continue to stimulate with an invigorating body scrub, using a sisal washcloth or mitt and an uplifting scented gel, such as bergamont, lemon grass, or grapefruit. Place a small amount of the gel in a wet cloth or mitt and rub it all over your body, using an upward motion. The gentle exfoliation of this revitalizing rub will give skin a healthy looking morning glow.

❖ **Invigorating Shower:** Once you've finished cleansing, decrease the temperature of the shower until its cool and rinse for 15 seconds, then adjust the temperature back to warm for one or two minutes. The transition from warm to cold stimulates blood flow, which exercises the capillary walls and tones tissues while encouraging stimulation.

❖ **Energizing Mist:** Towel yourself dry and to energize mist your body with a mixture of five ounces distilled water, one teaspoon of olive oil and three drops each rosemary and cypress essential oils (you may add a sprig of fresh rosemary if you like) blended together in a misting bottle (you'll need to shake it well), The olive oil moisturizes your skin while rosemary is energizing and cypress stimulates circulation. Allow this "morning dew" to air-dry on your body. (Other energizing oils include grapefruit, lemon and orange.)

Phase 7: Refresh (Protect your face)

Our faces have to cope with a lot of problems, from damaging free facials - found in pollution, cigarette smoke, and pesticides - to oiliness and everyday stress, all of which take their toll on skin. Don't despair.

Daily cleansing and care helps manage troubled skin. Antioxidants such as vitamins A, C, and E are powerful allies that can help protect against free-radical damage.

The basic steps of face care are valid for any skin care regimen. Everyone's skin is unique and it's important to use products that compliment your skin type. Treatments that contain tee tree oil are especially good for oily and acne prone skin.

Tee tree oil has been called a first aid kit in a bottle. Historically, tea tree oil has been used to treat everything from sunburns and stings to gum infections and athlete's feet. It's deep cleansing and anti-bacterial properties make it especially good for controlling blemishes.

What you'll need: facial cleanser, facial scrub, hot water, rose essential oil, vitamin C moisturizer and a fluffy towel.

- ❖ **Tee Tree Wash and Exfoliation:** Splash your face with tepid water. Using a tea tree face wash, massage the cleanser all over your face and neck, using small circular motions. Rinse with tepid water. Use a gentle scrub, one that contains tee tree oil as an active ingredient, to further cleanse and exfoliate your skin. Once again use gentle circular motions as you exfoliate and deeply cleanse your face, rinse again with tepid water.

- ❖ **Oil Control Mask:** Spread a thin, even layer of a tee tree-based facial mask over your face, avoiding the lip and eye areas. Leave the mask on for ten minutes, (these asks do not generally dry to the touch) then remove the mask by splashing your face with warm water and wiping away the mask with your fingers or a moistened cotton pad.

❖ **Moisturizing Gel:** Even if you have oily skin, be careful of over drying. Oily skin needs moisturizing, too. A tea tree moisturizing gel softens and hydrates your skin without irritation, while antibacterial agents help soothe blemishes. Apply a quarter-sized squeeze of gel to your fingers and massage it gently into your skin.

❖ **Antioxidant Cleanse:** Wet your face and disperse a dime-sized amount of facial cleanser onto two fingers (try one with vitamin C). Rub your fingers together, using gentle circular motions. Massage the cleaner over your entire face and neck. Always rinse with tepid water and pat your face dry. (Hot water can damage tiny blood tissues)

❖ **Face Scrub:** Gently exfoliate your skin to remove dead cells, impurities and sebum, speeding cell renewal and allowing smooth new skin to shine. Use a small dollop of your favorite facial scrub (fruit based facial scrubs are a good choice as their natural enzymes are great defoliators). Lightly rub your fingers in circles over the entire face, avoiding the eye area. Rinse and pat dry.

❖ **Essential Steam:** Fill a large bowl with boiling water. Add three drops rose essential oil agitate the water to activate the oil and release its vapors. Lean over the bowl keeping your face 10 to 12 inches away from the water. Put a bath towel over your head and tent it around the bowl to trap the vapors. Steam your face for 5 to 10 minutes. Rose oil helps irritated or dry skin; use lavender essential oil for dry-to-normal skin, or lemon for oily skin. (Note the rose essential oil is quite expensive so most commercially available oils are diluted.)

❖ **Vitamin C Mask and Moisturizer:** A vitamin C mask can help restore the skin's lipid barrier, the intercellular material the regulates the flow of water through skin layers. Spread a small amount over your face in a thin, even layer; leave it on for 10 to 20 minutes, then remove it with a wet cloth and pat dry. Apply a vitamin C moisturizer while your skin is still damp to seal in moisture and fortify skin.

Phase 8: Infusion (Take the waters)

The word spa comes from the Latin phrase *salus per aquam*, "health via water." Hydrotherapy is the basis of European, *kurs,* mineral water-based treatments that incorporate hot and cold soaks, baths, steam, showers, and drinking of mineral water to help aid specific ailments. Create this experience in your bath to tap into the health benefits of water.

What you'll need: sugar scrub, mineral bath salts and a towel.

❖ **Sugar Scrub:** Take a five-minute hot water shower to soften your skin. Turn off the shower, and using a handful of sugar scrub; gently rub it over your skin, beginning at your neck (avoid your face) and working down to your feet. Rinse off the sugar with warm water, then slowly decrease the temperature and stand in a cool spray for a minute or two, to prepare for a hot soak. Pat yourself dry.

❖ **Mineral Bath:** For centuries, Europeans have *"taken the waters,"* soaking in and drinking mineral water from local hot springs for their curative benefits. Even the water in the home bath can offer good benefits; simply fill the tub high enough to immerse your body completely. Add 1/2 cup of your favorite mineral bath salts to the water and mix them until they completely dissolve. Ease into the tub, lie back, close your eyes and rest for at least twenty minutes. Breathe slowly and deeply.

❖ **Resting Wrap:** A rest period is the most important step of a bathing ritual. During this time your parasympathetic nervous system works to restore your body. Spread a couple of heavy blankets over a chair (use a soft blanket on top since it will be in contact with your body). Remove your robe and lie on the blankets, wrapping them comfortably around your body. Rest while wrapped for twenty or thirty minutes.

Phase 9: Refining (Help your hands)

A woman's hands are exposed to the elements daily from washing dishes to typing emails. Great looking hands and nails make a strong impression and so do troubled ones. If your hands are dry, your nails are brittle or uneven, or your cuticles are hard and curling, its time for some hand help. Overworked hands need care and attention to look their best. (See Nail Care)

What you'll need: lavender essential oil, cuticle cream.

❖ **Soak The Hands:** Soak your hands with warm water. Add 2 drops of lavender essential oil. Lavender acts as a soothing antibacterial agent, helping to clean and disinfect nail beds. Immerse the tip of your fingers into the water making sure your nails and cuticles are completely covered. Soak for five minutes. This softens the cuticles and helps prepare the nails for additional care. Apply cuticle cream on a regular basis.

❖ **Exfoliation and Grooming:** Exfoliate with your favorite scrub, working from the top of your hand up your fingers to the nails and around the cuticles. Rinse; then with an emery board (metal files can damage nails), file each nail from one side to the center with one smooth movement and repeat from the other side. Push back cuticles using an orange stick wrapped in a small piece of cotton (never cut your cuticles, as this can cause infection).

❖ **Hydrating Massage:** Your hands have fewer oil glands than the skin on the rest of your body. Apply an extensive restorative lotion, such as vitamin E or hemp to keep them well hydrated. Disperse a small amount in your hands and rub them together to spread the lotion evenly. While hydrating your skin, give yourself a simple massage to help relieve hand fatigue. With your thumb, rub deeply in small cuticles all over your palm and along the length of each finger.

❖ **Nail Buffing:** Finish your manicure by giving your nails a natural shine, using a buffing file or block. Hold the buffer between your thumb and finger; curl the fingers of your other hand in toward your palm. Slightly extend one finger at a time and use the buffer in a back and forth motion across each nail, using quick, smooth strokes to give nails a long lasting polished shine.

Phase 10: Foot Care: (Pamper Your Feet)

A pedicure is not a luxury. Your feet deserve to be treated at least as well as the rest of your body. Warm water and salts soothe tired and sore muscles caused by high heels, new shoes, or long days on your feet. Exfoliation lifts off layers of dead skin cells and accelerates cell renewal, keeping your skin soft and smooth. Foot detox helps circulate blood and reduces pain in you body.

If you'd like to do some serious pampering, treat yourself to a sugar or salt scrub, foot detoxification, feet massage, hot wax hydration dip, or overnight hydration and peppermint foot lotion and foot mitts or socks.

What you'll need: peppermint oil, crystals, pumice stone, emery board, peppermint, tee tree essential oil, mint leaves, foot roller, towel, foot file, shea butter, foot bootie/cotton socks, and moisturizer.

- ❖ **Peppermint Foot Soak:** Peppermint cools, refreshes and energizes. This soothing soak begins with a warm sensation that turns into a cool tingle. Begin by filling a large bowl with warm water so that the water level is just below your ankles, and then add one-tablespoon peppermint oil minerals crystals. Soak your feet for at least ten minutes to soften and refresh your skin, making exfoliation easier and more effective.
- ❖ **Peppermint Foot Mask:** To really refresh and hydrate your feet. Finish with a peppermint foot mask. Scoop out the mask

and spread a thick layer over your feet, covering the tops and soles as well as in between your toes. Do not rub the mask in. Leave the mask n for 15 minutes, then remove it with a wet washcloth or rinse your feet in a tub.

❖ **Pumice Smoothing and Grooming:** To smooth the skin on your heels, use a pumice stone after a foot soak. Grasp the pumice stone in one hand and firmly rub it up and down from the back of your heel to the bottom of your foot. Continue until the skin feels smooth. Repeat on your other foot. Dry your feet thoroughly, especially between your toes. To groom your toenails, cut them straight across, filing any short edges. Then just as you would with your fingernails, gently push back your cuticles with a cotton-wrapped orange stick. You can also buff your toenails for a healthy looking shine.

❖ **Cucumber Mint-Soak:** Fill a large basin with cold water. Add six drops tee tree essential oils; add a sliced cucumber and a handful of torn fresh mint leaves to the water. Place the basin at the foot of your favorite chair and ease your feet into the water. Tee tree oil has antibacterial properties and cucumber has a mild astringent, mint gives your feet a fresh scent. Soak for 15 minutes and dry your feet.

❖ **Foot Roller Rub:** Place your right foot on a wooden foot massage roller. Press your feet against the roller and move it forward and back over the roller, varying the speed and pressure. Continue massaging for 5 to 10 minutes, then switch feet, but also to massage the four-reflexology zones of the foot. When pressed, these zones affect corresponding parts of the

- ❖ body, the head and neck, chest and shoulders, vital organs and lower abdomen and pelvis.

- ❖ **Wrap and Rest:** Wrap your feet in a towel, elevate them, and relax for 10 minutes. Wrapping your feet keeps them warm prompting for complete relaxation. And deep absorption of the lotion and ensuring maximum hydration. Elevating tired feet and ankles reduce fluid retention and helps improve circulation.

- ❖ **Heel Filing:** While your feet are still damp, use a foot file to remove hard, dead skin. Most people have hard skin on their heels; other likely spots include the balls of the feet; the bottoms of your big toes, and the tops of your little toes. Using a firm back-and-forth motion, file the hard skin of these points. Stop filing every few strokes to feel your skin; when it no longer feels rough, move on to the next area (stop at any sign of pain). If your feet are severely dry and cracked it may take several treatments to smooth them.

- ❖ **Overnight Foot Hydration:** Hydrate your newly pampered feet with shea butter balm or other body butter or an intensive moisturizer such as hemp oil or deep penetrating lotion. Leaving a heavy application of moisturizer on overnight can have a dramatic effect on dry skin. Apply the balm generously to one foot then cover it with a deep moisturizing foot bootie (you can use a cotton sock if you don't have a bootie). Repeat with your other foot then leave the booties on overnight.

Phase 11: Foot Detoxification (Footbath)

One of the newest ways of cleansing the body is the Ionic Cleanse Foot Detox. Obesity and health related diseases are at epidemic proportions in our country and despite all efforts we, as women continue to gain weight. The reason may be related to our toxin overload more than our calories.

Body fat accumulation, especially around the middle section, is a visible sign of toxic build up and a good indication that the liver is not functioning as effectively as it should. This "body garbage", along with toxins and heavy metals, also clogs organs, tissues and lymph systems.

Your struggles with losing weight are not simply the result of too much food and not enough exercise. Toxins and debris the body cannot eliminate are stored in fatty tissue, joints, muscles, and the brain. This leads to excess weight that diet and exercise can't change.

The Complete Detox System helps you to lose weight, reduce cellulite and have healthy, glowing skin by cleaning out your body in a most unique way. This stimulates your lymph system and draws out toxins, cellular waste and pollutants from the body.

The detox footbaths operate through the process of electrolysis. This generates current in the foot bath water causing molecules of H20 to divide producing negative ions. A negative ion is an atom that has lost or gained electrons causing it to become negatively charged. The negative ion is smaller than a molecule, which allows it to be easily absorbed by the body through the process of osmosis. As your body absorbs energy from the water it stimulates the Lymphatic System by breaking the ionic bond of toxins clogging it, which allows them to be pulled from the body through the pores in the feet. Once the lymph system begins to clear, it again starts draining toxins into the GI Tract where more toxins are released. It also increases T-Cell production giving the immune system more of them to use for fighting illness.

To really refresh and detox your body hydrate your feet. The ionic water footbath cleanses balances and enhances the bio-energy. While the footbath is widely used to increase energy, vitality, and stamina, at the same time, it purges (detoxifies) the body of toxins, chemicals, radiation, pollution, synthetics, and other foreign material trapped in the skin layers that have clogged up the body's systems of elimination. For more details visit the World Wide Web or contact an ionic cleanse foot detox specialist. One of my favorites is **BJ's**. She can be reached at 214.566.8621. She loves to pamper your feet and your spirit.

What you'll need: Good spirit and an open mind. Your detox specialist will provide everything else.

Phase 12: Purify (Cleanse impurities)

A body is a woman's temple, but sometimes the way women treat their bodies is less than holy. Unhealthy habits or neglect can leave a woman in real need of purification. For centuries, mud has been used to detoxify the body and remineralize skin. Mud can help draw out impurities, smooth and clarify skin, restoring its purity.

Giving yourself a full body mud treatment is not always an option. With mudpacks you can reap the benefits of mud while using only what you need where you need it.

As far back as 120B.C., the Roman used mud as remedies to heal wounds. Today mud is used in European spas to aid conditions such as arthritis and rheumatism as well as for injuries such as pulled muscles. A mudpack is placed directly on the problem area, such as the knee, back elbow, or wrist. The heat combined with the chemical makeup of the mud can be powerfully effective.

What you'll need: body mud, 6-8 large towels, body brush, nail brush, Olive oil or shea butter, detoxifying beverage or tonic.

❖ **Mud Warming:** When making mudpacks, you'll need a thick body mud that does not run. With a spatula, scoop a cup of mud in a small heat conductive towel. Boil some water and fill a larger bowl with boiled water. Place the small bowl into the larger bowl of hot water to warm it; stir the mud occasionally as heats. If it's easier you may also heat the mud in the bowl placed in a pan of hot water or in a double boiler in your stovetop.

❖ **Making the Mudpack:** Cut a piece of very porous cloth (heavy gauze or cheesecloth) into a 12 by 12 inch square and place the cloth on the table. When the mud is hot, remove it from the water; with a spatula, scoop all of the mud out of the bowl onto the center of the cloth and mound it so that it's about an inch or two thick in the center. Fold each corner of the cloth in on top of the mud to form a pack.

❖ **Making Your Mudpack Mist:** In a misting bottle blend two cups of distilled water with five drops of Rosemary and five drops of orange essential oils (these help promote detoxification). Shake well and spray on mud until moist - when needed.

- **Mud Application:** This ritual is especially enjoyable outside on a warm day, but it can also be done in your bathroom - just be prepared for a little more clean up. Using your favorite body mud, cover your entire body. Include your face if you like, but be careful to avoid the eye and lip area. It is not necessary for the mud application to be thick.

- **Spot Treatments:** Position the mudpack directly on any area causing discomfort. Make sure to keep the folded layers of cloth on the top of the pack and the thin porous layer against your skin. Wind some plastic wraparound the affected area to retain the heat, and then cover it with a towel. Leave the packs wrapped for twenty to thirty minutes. The minerals, vitamins and plant substances found in some mud's may be absorbed through the skins surface into the body clearing metabolic pathways, improving waste elimination, cell oxygenation, and nerve function and easing aching muscles.

- **Drying and Purifying:** When you have finished applying the mud, relax on the lounge or a bed covered with plenty of towels while the mud begins to dry (some of the mud will automatically rub off so cover the bed good). As the mud dries you'll feel your skin tightening. Many mud's help draw out impurities and toxins and temporarily tone your skin. After 15 minutes refresh the mud mask with a body mist. It tends to feel more comfortable if kept moist, so spray it as needed.

- **Warm Rinsing:** When the mud has dried again (about 15 minutes after misting) rinse off in a warm shower. Simply use your hands or a washcloth to wipe away the mud. It may take a few minutes to remove it all (you may want to use a nail brush to help clean your hands and feet). Do not use any soap or cleaners. They wash away beneficial trace minerals that are there to help restore the skin.

❖ **Emollient Moisturizing:** Once you have rinsed away all the mud, pat yourself dry. Using a rich body butter containing an intensive emollient such as olive oil or shea butter. Spread the butter evenly over the body and rub it in. (Do not use the product on your face, it may be too rich). Enjoy a detoxifying beverage or tonic to further cleanse your system.

Phase 13: Toning (Love your face

Aging is a four-letter word to every woman in our society. LOVE! People spend millions of dollars each year on chemical peels, face-lifts, and Botox injections in hopes of retaining the illusion of youth. Don't buy into that buzz. Natural toned skin is beautiful at any age.

Maintain good skin tone using vitamins, acupressure, and aromatic essential oils. We can't turn back the hands of time, but we can care for the faces we love.

What you'll need: vitamin E skin cleaner, vitamin E lotion, and 5 mediums sized smooth stones.

❖ **Cream Cleansing:** Cleansing is the most important element of facial skin care. Unless skin is thoroughly cleansed on a daily basis it will look dull and lifeless. A mild vitamin E cream cleaner is great for gently washing away make-up pollutants and other skin dulling residues. Wet your skin with plain warm water and dispense a quarter-sized amount of cleanser onto your fingers; apply it evenly to your face. Massage vitamin E lotion into your skin with your fingertips using gentle circular motions, rinse and pat dry with a soft towel.

❖ **Acupressure Facial Toning:** With the middle finger braced behind your index fingers, press firmly and massage the following points: Making six tiny circles at each point directly between your eyebrows. Circle left one inch above the arches of both eyebrows. Circle inward; the fronts of both temples. Circle outward on both cheekbones, just under the edges of your eyes. Circle outward on either side of your nose at the inner bases of the cheekbones. Circle outward, between your nose and upper lip. Circle right between your lower lip. Circle the bottom of your chin circling right.

❖ **Warm Stone Treatment:** Place three medium-sized smooth flat stones in a bowl of hot water. Warm them for about ten minutes, then dry them, Lie on a comfortable surface on your back and place one stone below your hairline in the middle of your forehead. Place another between your eyebrows. Place the third between your bottom lip and the end of your chin.

The stones help warm acupressure points on your face, releasing muscle tension and stimulating nerves. Relax and breathe slowly and deeply leaving the stones on your face until they have cooled.

Phase 14: Defend (Boost immunity)

If you feel you might be catching something or if last night's hectic schedule is catching up with you, instead of heading to the medicine cabinet, consider a natural and relaxing remedy.

A simple body wrap can help open the airways, soothe muscles, aid in your immune system and eliminate impurities. Plus you get some much-needed rest while supporting your body's incredible ability to restore itself.

What you'll need: 5 medium sized massage stones, eucalyptus oil, 2 large bowls or pans, Rosemary oil, 2 large bath towels, 2 heavy blanket, 2 flat bed sheets, skin lotion, peppermint Eucalyptus or tea tree lotion, one cup distilled water, sage, misting bottle, soft pillow.

❖ **Aromatic Steam:** Fill a bowl with massage stones and dispense five drops, eucalyptus essential oils into it. Place the bowl on a shelf in or on the floor of the shower, away from the direct stream of water. Let the hot water run for a few minutes to activate the oil and build up steam. As the shower heats up fill another large bowl or pan with hot water and add three drops Rosemary essential oil. Place a bath towel in it and let it soak (you'll use this to prepare the body wrap). Adjust the water temperature. Enter the shower, and relax for ten minutes in the warm water and scented steam.

❖ **Invigorating Hydration:** Dry off and use an upward motion while applying an invigorating skin lotion to your body to hydrate your skin and stimulate your lymphatic system. Try a peppermint Eucalyptus or tea tree lotion. To warm the lotion leave the dispenser in hot water as you're showering. When performing lymphatic stimulation, always stroke lightly and toward the heart.

❖ **Herbal Infusion:** Soak a bath sized towel in rosemary infused water. Lay two heavy blankets out on a bed or chaise and spread a sheet over the blankets. Remove the towel from the rosemary infused water, wringing it out and laying it over the sheet. Using a solution of one cup distilled water and three drops each sage and rosemary essential oils (you may also add a sprig of fresh rosemary), lightly mist the sheets.

❖ **Resting Wrap:** Place a soft pillow where your head will rest. Lay on top of the blankets, sheet and hot towel, then wrap the sheet and both blankets tightly around the torso, legs and feet. Position the pillow comfortably behind your head and neck, making sure your feet are elevated. Rest for twenty of thirty minutes.

Phase 15: Restore (Bounce back)

Whether you're a weekend warrior or a professional athlete, you demand great things from your body. To keep functioning at your peak you need to be as good to your body as it is to you. Soak, heat, rub, and rest it as often as you can. A few minutes of self-care can make a big difference, not only in performance, but also in overall well-being.

What you'll need: peppermint essential oil, lemongrass essential oil, small bowl, stool or chair, reflex ball or golf ball.

❖ **Aromatic Steam Bath:** Put four drops each peppermint and lemongrass essential oils into a small bowl and place it on a ledge or on to the floor of a steamy shower, away from the water steam. Allow the steam to activate the oils for a minute. Turn the water temperature down a bit and relax in the shower for ten minutes.

❖ **Foot Roll:** Sitting on a stool or chair, place the reflex ball under your right foot (you may also use a golf ball) Lean on the foot, putting pressure on the ball. Roll your foot up and down over the ball, this not only relaxes your feet, but also stimulate the reflexology points that correspond to the other parts of your body. Flex your foot then point your toe as you roll. Grip and squeeze the ball with your toes. Repeat with other foot. Work each foot for five minutes.

Phase 16: Immersing Within (Find peace)

Bathing is so scared in Japan that you are required to cleanse before you enter the bath or hot spring. Socializing is as much a part of the ritual as is scrubbing and cleansing. When there's a need for peace and serenity, women retreat to their home tubs. You can create a Zen bathing experience; all you need is the right state of mind.

What you'll need: loofah, bath soap or gel, shampoo, thick towel, candle-pampering aromatherapy diffuser, sage, high quality loose green tea leaves, teapot, myrrh, frankincense, or sandalwood.

❖ **Loofah Scrubbing:** Turn on your shower and adjust the water to tepid (a soak is a later part of this ritual, so begin with a cooler shower). Hold a loofah under the shower stream until it is pliable. Using your favorite bath soap or gel, gently scrub your entire body (except your face). Use upward strokes, working toward your heart. You may shampoo your hair if you wish. When you're finished scrubbing, get out of the shower and pat your body dry with a thick towel.

❖ **Aromatherapy Diffusion:** Draw a hot bath - not scalding, but hot enough that you'll have to ease in very slowly. While the bath is filling, light a candle-pampering aromatherapy diffuser and place it on the floor next to the bath so that the scent will travel past where you rest your head. Choose an essential oil known for its ability to bring your body into balance and restore your physical and emotional equilibrium, such as clay sage, myrrh, frankincense, or sandalwood. Once the bath is filled, turn off the water and ease into the tub.

❖ **Tea Ritual:** In Japan the tea ritual is seen as a way to escape the stresses of the day-to-day living and experience inner peace. Put some high quality loose green tea leaves in a tea ball; place the ball in a teapot and pour simmering water over it. Let it steep for three to six minutes. Focus on your inner tranquility as you enjoy this healthy brew. Non-fermented teas are high in antioxidants.

Phase 17: Retreatment (Drifting off)

A good night's sleep is delicious and essential for our mental and physical health. Sometimes we're so wound up we can't manage to drift off, and the minutes tick by as we lie awake. Just as you'd prepare for waking activities, try preparing for sleep. Make time to soothe yourself. Sleep can't be forced; relax as you approach.

What you'll need: lavender and chamomile essential oils, candles, towel

❖ **Relaxing Baths:** Draw a warm bath. Do not make it too hot. You should be able to enter the bath comfortably and remain in it for half an hour. After the bath fills, add 10 to 20 drops each lavender and chamomile essential oils, and agitate the water with your hand to mix. Light some candles around the tub and turn off the lights. Enter the tub and lie back. Close your eyes and slowly run your thoughts through your mind. Whenever you find tension, consciously try to release it. Soak for 30 minutes, letting go of every day stress.

❖ **Deep Belly Breathing:** This kind of breathing can be very calming. After one of your baths; lie comfortably in bed on your back. Breathe in deeply through your nose, filling your lungs to the full capacity; your upper chest should rise as your lungs fill. Exhale through your mouth. Listen to your breath as you exhale. Next, as you inhale through your nose, focus on breathing into your abdomen as well as your chest. Exhale through your mouth. Repeat this pattern for up to 100 breaths, or until you fall asleep.

❖ **Sleep Inducer:** Soak in tea instead of drinking it before going to bed. Steep four bags each of tangerine lavender and chamomile tea in a pot of boiling water. Add this mixture to your bath and submerge yourself in the tub. Close the room up to seal in the steamed aroma. Relax for ten minutes or more as you inhale the scents. You'll be able to fall asleep sooner after the sleep inducer bath.

Other Baths That Pamper

Bathing serves a dual purpose, one for cleansing and also for therapeutic purposes. Bathing has become the fabulous lost ritual that deserves to be redefined in every woman's life. Bathing has always been the divine power and a gift to be revered and respected.

Water is the most healing of all remedies and the best of all cosmetics. To treat water carelessly is to neglect an important part of your pampering process. Water is considered to be sacred in almost every culture. Royalty enjoys daily baths for hours at a time. Bathing is a ritual appearing in many cultures and is revealed in many sacred writings of India and the Middle East.

Baptism by water is sacred in many religions. In the 15th century Knights of the Bath were ceremoniously bathed for purity of the spirit. In Ancient Rome baths took almost six hours. Oils and balsams are used to make baths more alluring and inviting. The entire bathing ritual was an eight step process that concluded with oiling and perfuming the body with best fragrances affordable.

What you'll need: grated ginger root, fresh mint leaves, cinnamon, champagne, your favorite appetizers, tangerine lavender chamomile tea, Epsom salt, baby oil, teaspoon of dry mustard, thyme, and lavender, pumice stone, candles, music and champagne.

❖ **Aphrodisiac Bath:** Turn your tub into foreplay; invite him to join you in a bath spiked with two to three tablespoons of grated ginger root, fresh mint leaves and cinnamon. For an added arousing effect, feast on champagne and your favorite appetizers.

❖ **At Home Salt Glow:** Prepare a grainy mixture of two cups of Epsom salt and one cup of baby oil. Set the mixture aside and soak in plain warm water from ten to fifteen minutes, then stand up and rub concoction onto legs, arms, belly, back and buttocks. Rinse in the shower, dry off skin and smooth on more baby oil.

❖ **After Sports Muscle Relaxer:** After a good work out to ease muscle spasms or tightness, spice warm tub with a teaspoon of dry mustard, thyme, and lavender.

❖ **Champagne Bath:** This is more erotic when bathing with your lover. Bring a chilled bottle of champagne to your hot tub or bath. As you bathe sip the champagne slowly. Be sure to finish the bottle in thirty to forty minutes. During this time dream up the most pampered things you're going to do to your lover. Just talking and laughing adds to the pleasures of the champagne bath. Pouring small trickles down his back or on his chest while bathing is quite refreshing.

Special Reminder:

Listen to your body. Stop if you feel uncomfortable. If you are pregnant or have a chronic illness seek advice from your physician prior to any spa bath or product, especially if you chose essential oils. Read all directions on product labels thoroughly prior to use.

- ❖ Prior to applying products to skin, do a patch test and check for allergies. Aapply a small amount of the product to area of your skin to make sure there's no adverse reaction.

- ❖ Do not use exfoliating products or tools on irritated skin. Test the temperature of water to avoid burns.

- ❖ Oils are used throughout this book. Because essential oils are very potent, never drink them or apply them to diluted oils or directly to your skin unless specifically instructed to do so.

- ❖ Soak no longer than twenty minutes, to prevent dehydrating

- ❖ The best water temperature is 85 degrees

- ❖ Use a clean pumice stone on feet.

- ❖ Use loofah the knees, elbows, and bikini line. You'll feel like silk when he touches you.

- ❖ Moisturize immediately after bathing. It seals in water that skin has absorbed taking years off of aging skin.

- ❖ Lavish yourself with care. Enjoy yourself to the fullest. Forget all the negatives and lift your spirits.

Cool-water baths are refreshing
Cold-water baths are invigorating.
Warm-water baths are soothing.
Hot-water baths are relaxing.

13

Host a 'Girl's Night In' Pamper Party

Good times, good friends, good food, good drinks…

What more could a girl ask for.

P amper Parties! ... Get together with a few of your good friends, a few bottles of good wine, and some healthy appetizers. Add soothing music, relaxing massages, beauty treatments, great conversation and the good times are wonderfully invigorating ways to spend an evening with your best girlfriends.

It's about midnight on a Friday, and lavender aromatherapy scents fill the air. The party is going strong. Wine, champagne, sparkling water, cold drinks, fresh vegetables, cheese, sliced fruit assorted meats and seafoods are spread out on a table.

Here's an example. The sounds of soothing instrumental music and voices of happy women fill the air. One woman is feeling so good she's closed her eyes. Her head is cushioned, her feet are being massaged and a joyous smile is planted on her face.

Another is stretched out on a massage table - lying in a semi-dark private room, enjoying a firm pair of hands that are working methodically over all parts of her stressed body.

Two other women are experiencing soothing mud pack facials. Another is wrapped in a fluffy white bathrobe and stretched out on a lounger with cucumbers on her eyes.   There's another woman sitting with headphones on her head with hot paraffin wax moisturizer on her hands and feet.

Four others are relaxing with their hair wrapped in towels and their feet soaking in basins of warm, scented water. "Mmmm," one sighs. *"This is simply divine."* Another one moans, *"God knows I needed this."*

Welcome to the latest embodiment of girls' night out: *'the girl's night in'* pamper party. By day, these women lead busy lives. One is a homemaker and mother of five children, one works in a doctor's office, one works for the largest air conditioning company in the world, one runs a catering company. Another is a flight instructor and another is an hotelier. So to relieve stress they gather every few months at one of their homes, put on soft music, change clothes and let massage therapists and other professionals work their magic.

"It's more intimate than a health spa," says Marva, the flight instructor. "And your time is not limited. It's very stimulating to get together with other women to discuss pampering, men, relationships, goals and to network."

Day spas are recognizing this *girl's night in trend* by offering mobile services. Added to this is an expanding array of do-it-yourself kits sold in stores nationwide with everything from aromatherapy candles to body scrubs, and it's clear that home spa treatments are becoming more popular.

The setting can be luxurious (a hotel suite with a fleet of beauty technicians) or intimate (a few friends giving one another facials at your home). Some pamper parties have included as many as 20 women, but there are many ways to enjoy them and scale down the cost.

'Girls Night In' Pamper Party Formula

Unwind, relax and distress with the aid of a therapist, give your girlfriends a range of complimentary therapies. Choose from the following types of spa treatments. (See also Spa Treatments and Benefits in the back of this book.)

Indian head massage	Aromatherapy Body massage
Hot stone massage	Indonesian massage
Ayurvedic therapy	Hopi ear candles
Holistic facial	Holistic pedicure Reflexology
Cupping	Reiki
Tibetan head massage	Thai seated massage
Korean hand massage	Algae body wrap
Ayurvedic leg/foot ritual	Indian spice body polish

It is really up to you to choose the type of pampering treatments that you or your guests will appreciate. A massage helps relax your guests and can be accompanied by beauty treatments or complimentary therapies.

Many spas bring every element of the spa to you, with a custom menu of pampering for your group. Enjoy luxurious treatments in the comfort and convenience of your home with the same sensory details that you experience in a spa - aromatherapy, relaxing music, candles, robes and slippers.

In addition, you can give a spa gift of an aromatherapy candle and either bath salts, neroli mist or foot balm. It's up to you!

How To Host A Pamper Party

You can choose to host the party as a gift to your best friends or family members or have everyone select and pay for their own services. It's as simple as sending out an invitation, taking everyone's spa treatment order and taking care of everything by creating a schedule for the technicians, sending the correct number of people and spacing out the appointments so that you have ample time to relax and chat.

Pamper Parties can include express facials, 30 minute massages, manicures, and pedicures or the works which might include a series of treatments for each person. Make sure they last long enough for your guests to simultaneously beautify and socialize.

Mixing A Pamper Party with A Book Party!

You can combine a pampering party with a book club party. This can really make your pampering party fun.' Here's how to do it.

- Issue invites to your party by sending them out attached to your bestseller *Pampering Pleasures or Sexual Healing.*
- Instruct everyone read the book before they come to the party.
- Use decorations that reflect the theme of the book.
- Use homemade bookmarks as napkin holders.
- Read a chapter together at the party. (The host gets to select the featured chapter.)
- A mother-daughter Pamper-Book Club party is a great idea too. Be sure to choose a chapter that both of you will enjoy.
- Use elegant gloves as napkin holders. Place the napkins half way inside the gloves.
- To keep conversation going use a beautiful purse to hold questions about the book. Pass the purse along to each guest to get everyone involved. Guests can place their questions in the purse upon arrival.
- Provide bookmarkers as gifts or guests can create their own.
- Have the each guest write his or her initial on a piece of felt with a marker. Later, you can hand stitch their initials to give at the next book club gathering.
- Coordinate the activities so that they flow smoothly and every guest gets equal amounts of pampering.

"Look at everything as though you were seeing it either for the first or last time. Then your time on earth will be filled with glory."
- Betty Smith

14

Creating a Home Where You Feel Nurtured, and Pampered

Your home should display an inviting, neat, clean and wholesome

environment.

A woman's home is her shelter. It's her safe haven and a place for her to find happiness, peace and comfort. It's a reflection of her soul, who she is and what she values. It reflects bits and pieces of her sensitivities. Pampering is more about the spirit of the woman.

This chapter discusses many of the methods that help women tap into all five senses and shows how each sense can provide the stimuli to create a wonderfully pampered home.

Have you ever walked into a home and it felt so good being there that you uttered ... Ummmmm? Have you ever saw someone's home and wished it were yours? Did you like the sensitivity within it? Could you feel the love and nurturing in it? Did you like the smell, feel, sound and sight of it? Have you ever seen a home so beautiful that your thoughts begin to move in a happy direction? Did you want to relax after seeing and feeling a pampered home? Did it make you feel warm and cozy on your insides? Did you wish it were yours?

Your home can bring about these same feelings. Your home should be a sanctuary where you feel nurtured, refreshed, relaxed and pampered.

Ask yourself what it is you want your home to symbolize. Does it display the happiness you want? Is it inviting? Does it make you feel pampered? Does it have hints of love and affection scattered about each room? Is it comfortable? A better question might be what makes you really feel pampered? What kind of home would make you want to lie around all day?

Creating this sacred place is as easy as using your five senses. When you become aware of your surroundings and trust your instincts, you can turn your home or a special part of your home into a positive reflection of your soul.

Creating Your Own Pampered Sanctuary

Your home does not have to be expensively decorated to display neatness. Your goal should be to make your house a *home* by adding touches of comfort that personalizes your space.

Have you ever walked past a stranger who was wearing your favorite scent and thought, "Wow he smells good enough to eat? Or have you ever gotten goose bumps and felt tingly inside when you heard a song that reminded you of a past lover? Have you ever seen a man that looks so good you just had to say something to him? If you answered yes to any of these questions that means your senses kicked in during these times.

These are the same senses you'll use to create a home that's good enough to love. You'll achieve the look, smell, sight, sound and taste in your home that you want by creating the kind of home you really want.

Read on to find out how to make your house, apartment condo, ranch or whatever feels like a pampered Queen's paradise.

What Does Your Home Look Like?

What do you see as you walk up to the front door of your home? Do you see a comfortable and relaxing zone or a war zone? Does it make people who visit feel warm and welcome? Let's examine this a little further.

Start by painting your front door a welcoming color. Your entryway is the important transition between the outside world and your home. The color you choose should be warm, inviting and friendly. To add more personalization, place some colorful flowering plants on your front steps and hang positive flags that flutter gently in the breeze. Hang a sentimental welcome sign on your door to make your guests feel good.

Now, step over the threshold into the entryway to your home. Is it bright and joyful? Is it inviting? Is it calming and sensitive? Does it display peacefulness? Do your guests feel welcome? Is it clean? Is your entryway dark or dingy?

Try hanging brightly colored artwork or mirrors to reflect light. Different colors can evoke different feelings. Try to find soft, welcome colors that embody feelings of security and peace. Consider using blue for relaxation, yellow for energy, red for passion, and white for clarity. Keep this area clean and free of clutter.

What Does Your Home Sound Like?

Step inside; close your front door, stop and listen. Most people are surprised to discover that the ambient sound level in their homes is quite high. As you listen, consider what kinds of sounds you hear. Are they happy sounds such as birds chirping, joyful music or children playing? Is it the stressful noise of traffic or fussy neighbors? Is it the irritating noise of phones ringing, dogs barking or vehicle engines?

Your living room is where the outside world bursts in through telephones, televisions, radios and computers. Just as you wouldn't allow a boisterous guest to ruin the ambience, don't let the noise of the world overstay its welcome.

Create a retreat atmosphere by switching off everything that makes noise. Don't leave the television on if no one is watching and don't use it as background noise while you are busy elsewhere.

If you desire pleasant sounds here's an alternative. Play gentle music that can be heard upon entering your home. Be sure that you have a radio or stereo close by so that you can lounge with the sound of beautiful music in the background. Don't play anything too loud, or distracting, but rather soothing and pampering.

What Does Your Home Feel Like?

Walk into your home and look around. What do you feel upon entering? Does it feel safe, peaceful, happy and comfortable? Does it have the feeling of love and care? Does your lover enjoy the atmosphere of your home? Do people in general feel welcome and never want to leave? Does your guest feel comfortable? Are they at peace while in your home? Do you find that it takes a long time to say goodbye to guests or do they have a hard time leaving? If so, they probably like where they are. People are reluctant to leave a place where they feel calm, welcome, and warm.

Your home should display continuous comfort for others as well as yourself. It should display an inviting, and beautiful environment and it should always be a retreat from the outside world.

What Does Your Home Smell Like?

Your home is the perfect place to explore aromatherapy with bath salts, candles, oils and soaps. Quality, not quantity is important, so shop for pure oils, essences and beeswax candles with a pure cotton wick. Products containing pure oils and essences have stronger healing properties than those made from chemicals.

Research has shown that one of the fastest ways to influence mood is through smell. Some aromatherapy scents to consider: roses for romance, soothing aroma of vanilla for comfort, delicate scents of lavender, geranium or rosemary for relaxation, fresh fragrances of orange or peppermint for energy.

What Does Your Home Taste Like?

Your home is the place to celebrate life and nourishment. Honor your family heritage and create a dish similar to one you might experience while on a romantic date. Use all of your taste buds: sweet, sour, bitter, salty and taste textures such as crunchy, creamy or chewy.

Are you stuck in a taste rut with not enough zest in your food? Buy a new spice like cardamom or turmeric. Eat slowly, chew often and savor every bite of your food. Experiment by creating ethnic dishes together with good friends to nourish and to also sustain both your body and your spirit.

Continue to find ways to make your house an oasis of sensitivity and love by enhancing the environment. Include the man in your life as well as all who visit. Remember good food, good friends and good drinks bring good times.

Creating Ambience in Your Home

Remember ... creating your special place - a place of comfort and serenity - one that is personal and has everything you love is what makes your home reflect your taste.

Lighting: To set a relaxing and comforting mood, pay special attention to the lighting. Install a dimmer switch or place a small lamp in a corner. The shimmer and glitter of small bulbs from a chandelier can create a special atmosphere.

Candles: It's wonderful to set the mood for a romantic evening or decadent bath with flickering candles arranged on tables. In the bathroom place candles around the tub, on the counters, or even in cans on the floor. If you use scented candles, be sure not to mix too many fragrances. Find one you like and concentrate on one scent.

Bubble Baths: Have luxurious bubble bath or bath oil ready to pour into your water. The bubbles will look and feel fun, the oil will make your skin soft, and you'll feel so good you may never want to get out!

Towels: Be sure to invest in some wonderful, thirsty, thick, and large towels. When you get out, you'll be able to wrap yourself and hold the warmth inside. Invest in a luxurious terry or satin bathrobe to snuggle inside.

Lounge Chair: If your bathroom is large enough, consider putting a lounge chair, bench, or comfortable chair in the room. You'll be able to get out of the tub and not have to go to another room to sit down until you're ready.

To be honest a man doesn't really know a woman until he's seen her home. From the sofa to the rugs on the floor, each makes its own statement about who the woman is.

Your pampered happy home is your own and you'll want to cherish it and the things you bring into it.

Creating your pampered home is as easy as using your five senses: seeing, hearing, touching, smelling, and tasting.

15

Creating a Sensual Bedroom

Decide whether or not you want to be pampered or sexy, or both.

W alk into your bedroom and run your hand across your bedspread and pillows. Do they feel soft and inviting? Is your bedroom the kind of bedroom that makes you feel sexy, sensuous and pampered?

If you have difficulty falling asleep, even little things such as the feel and texture of sheets can have a big effect on how easily you doze off. Because you will spend nearly one-third of your life asleep your bedroom should be your place to renew at the beginning and relax at the end of each day.

Make your bed by using cool cotton sheets during spring and autumn. Use crisp linen sheets in summer for a peaceful sleep. Cuddly flannel sheets and fluffy down comforters create a cozy refuge in the wintertime. Lay plush carpeting and comfortable slippers to coddle your bare feet.

A woman's bedroom should be her temple of comfort, relaxation and intimacy. It should *not* be cluttered with items that have nothing to do with sleep or intimacy. Your bed should have a yummy feel as you cuddle or drift peacefully off to sleep.

Remove the dirty pile of laundry, put away the exercise gear, and hide the home computer. Bringing work and unnecessary items into the bedroom associates a woman's bedroom with all kinds of negative emotions – stress, work and clutter, etc. This is negative anchoring.

Your bedroom is an expression of who you are. Compliment it with furnishings and beautiful items that show cleanliness, coziness, care and concern. Everything placed in the bedroom whispers hints of what kind of personality you have and what kind of woman you really are. Is your bedroom decorated in a way that nothing about you shows in your environment? Is your personal flavor depicted in your surroundings? Take a look around and see what your bedroom says about you. Is it?

➢ Cluttered	➢ Insensitive
➢ Junky	➢ Warm
➢ Dirty	➢ Inviting
➢ Messy	➢ Conservative
➢ Cold	➢ Imaginative
➢ Drafty	➢ Sensitive

Looking at your bedroom can others see that you are a person that's …

➢ Caring	➢ Neat
➢ Family oriented	➢ Junky
➢ Faithful	➢ Messy

> ➤ Uncaring
> ➤ Religious

> ➤ Romantic
> ➤ Pet lover

Is scenery important to you? Are you cold or hot? Are you romantic or conventional? Are you a pack rat? Are you romantic? Are you pampered?

Starting today try to set goals that will help your bedroom stay pure and true. You should know what your bedroom says about you and become more tuned in to your own needs.

Replace the brightly lit lamps with flickering candles. Replace the dirty linens with fresh and clean ones and replace old, tattered and torn rugs with rich carpet. Change old outdated curtains or blinds with sheer, or lined to update window treatments. Place a collection of your favorite scents where the computer once was. Place beauty and self-care magazines around the room too. Potpourri, flowers and bright colored vases and candles help add beautiful touches here and there.

Add a few inexpensive things or your lover's favorite colors just to make him feel at home and welcome when he's in your environment. If the relationship doesn't work you can easily remove the items.

Over time, you and your lover will begin to associate good times, good smells and good things with your bedroom environment. If the pampered cues are powerful enough and the bedroom is free of negative anchors, you and your lover will experience an automatic and "positive trance" upon entering your bedroom.

Even if a woman lives in a small apartment or a home with limited space, she doesn't have to go crazy trying to make the perfect room. She should be practical and do what she can.

Where Are First & Last Impression Made?

Bedrooms are meant for sleeping, reading, reflecting, romancing, intimacy, recharging your batteries, and escaping from the cares of the day. Give your bedroom serenity and turn it into a private sanctuary by adding details and treatments that are personal and chic.

The quality of sleeping you receive every day in your bedroom is very important for your happiness, health and productivity. To create your perfect bedroom, you must think about what you like to do in your bedroom and define a style that's appropriate.

Consider your bedroom as a sacred retreat. It's very important that your connection with every object in your bedroom elicits a positive and nurturing response.

A cozy, bedroom atmosphere invites complete rest and rejuvenation of your body, mind and spirit. Cleanse your bedroom of items that keep negative memories and associations alive, and you'll find that it will become a place where you can embrace and revitalize your inner self.

The comfort and safety you feel in the world is directly connected to how safe and comfortable you feel in your home - bedrooms should be especially so.

Here is the place to plunge on fabrics that are sensual, including chenille, flannel, silk, cotton, satin, and velvet. Your view from the bed is very important, put a frame, a piece of art, a vase of flowers that inspire and makes you dream. The art in your bedroom makes a strong impact on your psyche too, so why not make it a positive one. Include sensual, serene or romantic images that calm and inspire you.

If you want to honor the five senses try focusing on creating a truly sensual environment. Whether single or coupled, your bedroom should be a place where all your senses are comforted and intimately celebrated. Light a scented candle, play music, and then relax. This is your oasis in which to celebrate the things you enjoy.

Create a Pleasing Bedroom Environment

Before retiring at night, consider writing in your journal, reading, or reflecting on your day, rather than watching television. If you have a television in your bedroom, store it in an armoire or cabinet when you're enjoying moments with your partner.

The bedroom often reflects a couple's relationship. Many couples don't realize that an environment can strengthen and nourish, or dampen and weaken, their intimacy. Place importance on your bedroom environment and connect in positive ways with one another.

The bedroom makes an impression. The more active or "crazy' a couple life's style is, the more crucial it is that they have a private and appealing bedroom sanctuary in which to, rejuvenate intimacy. Couples can nurture and enhance intimacy by thoughtfully creating a bedroom of allure, romance and celebration.

Planning a Bedroom for Happiness

The bedroom, with its softened textures, serene artwork, and muted patterns, intimately captures the warmth and essence of a home. Passion colors, such as red, purple, royal blue, rose, or the gilt of gold, add drama and indulgence.

Plan your bedroom design with private times in mind, beginning with the purpose of the bedroom. There are several important factors you should consider when trying to make an informed decision about the kind of bedroom you want. Let's discuss them.

Creating Your Bedroom Style

Define the style of bedroom you want. Comfort is the prevailing language of all well designed bedrooms. How it is translated and interpreted depends upon the individual. To some, soothing, soft and serene is comforting. To others, clean lined clarity is the most relaxing while still others find plush, sumptuous opulence the most blissful. Bedrooms are as individual as you are. To create yours, simply "follow your dreams" and use your personal likes to bring it to life.

Delighting Your Senses

What are some of the most enjoyable ways to soothe your senses? Consider sight, hearing, smell, touch, and taste? Make a list of what engages and delights each sense, and add to it as you think of new ideas. If you share a bedroom, ask your partner what he or she feels nurtured by, and incorporate those ideas as well. You should be struck with happiness each time the beautiful qualities of your bedroom come to mind.

Creating a Relaxed & Comforting Bedroom

Close your eyes and imagine the most comforting bedroom you can think of. Imagine a pile of fluffy pillows, a lofty down comforter, and stream of natural light warming the room, soft colors, patterns, blond wood floors, white sheer draperies swaying in the breeze. If this is the kind of bedroom you think about, the relaxed-style bedroom is for you.

The relaxed-style bedroom is made for sunny afternoon naps and leisure weekend mornings spent reading in bed. It is soft, nurturing and peaceful. The relaxed bedroom is perfectly suited for beachfront cottages or a cabin in the woods.

The relaxed bedroom is a celebration of simple and honest detail. All the senses are nurtured with the freshness and calmness of the room. Every element must be chosen for its ability to bring visual and emotional serenity to the space.

The floors should be soft underfoot with polished wood, scattered rugs, or natural sisal. The walls padded in sun-washed colors, may be covered with painted paneling, floral or striped papers, or satin-finished paint. Cool and tranquil, blue and white are classic color companions in a relaxed bedroom. A splash of bright sunny yellow or spring green brings warmth to the space and adds a touch of cheer.

The bed should be grand and impressive or low and understated. In either case, it is the linens that cover it and set the tone for the room. Buy quilted cotton, soft linen, and warm woolen blankets mixed and matched with downy pillows and cushy bolsters.

Windows welcome the outdoors in and when necessary, soft sheers, natural blinds, or painted shutters can provide privacy. Softly shaded lamps help illuminate the area with a peaceful glow. There are no fads or fashion criteria to the relaxed bedroom, only time that caresses with the ease and blissfulness of its style.

Creating Your Modern-Sophisticated Bedroom

For some people, the clean lines and uncluttered simplicity of the modern bedroom create a sanctuary that cannot be beaten. It is peaceful in its purity, refreshing in its refinement. Clutter is not welcome here.

Floors set the stage with cool concrete, light-tones polished woods, or structures carpets. The rule is sleek and spare. Walls become canvases of bold or demure colors and play host to expanses of glass, translucent doors, focused art, and architectural attributes.

The bed is often the modern-styled suite's focal point and, therefore, its style is very significant. Bedding should be tailored and simple. A sleigh bed of stainless steel, a cushioned armchair fashioned from stone will give a modern accent to your bedroom.

Furniture is selected to heighten the room's style. The importance of its design is only equaled by the function it serves. Window treatments, when necessary, are minimal and restrained; so are accessories. Bold statements of art, sculpture, and ingenious light fixtures are often the most fitting ways to accent the room while keeping it pristine and clean.

The trick is to remain focused on the simplicity and clarity of the space while being imaginative in its design details. Sophisticated bedroom welcomes you with a sense of elegance, a simple rich ambiance.

Mutes tones unify the elements of room surfaces, furnishings, and accents. The key to creating a sophisticated bedroom is simplicity. Soft natural shades of taupe, ivory, gray and brown most successfully accomplish this. A juxtaposition of materials flavors the room with a mix of rough and refined; linen plays against polished wood, glass pairs

116

with chiseled stone, and velvet teams with marble. Use texture rather than patterns to bring pampered rhythm and motion to the space. Lines of the furnishing should be round, keep them cleaned and uncluttered. A monochromatic color scheme on floors, walls, and ceilings, creates the ideal background.

Assorted woods may be paired; fabric and leathers of same tones should be combined. The interplay of tones and textures, rather than multiple colors and bold patterns, shapes the room's visual interest. Tailored window treatments are understated. Simple details like vases, pillows, lamps, candles, rug, art, and beautiful throws finish the room brilliantly.

Creating Your Exotic Bedroom

If you want a topical bedroom, all it takes are a venturesome spirit, a discerning eye, and imaginative details. Your bedroom can be a temporary escape from your daily routine as it transports you to some tropical island.

Choose a statement piece - a unique bed, distinctive piece of artwork or sculpture, or perhaps an exotic rug or fabric. You may choose a plantation style canopy bed, and then stylize it with bamboo flooring, grass-cloth wall coverings, and a large breezy ceiling fan. Use materials and colors indigenous – anything from cool seaside hues and bleached driftwood to spicy Mediterranean colors and chiseled stone.

Choose the accents and accessories, potted palms, tribal textiles, animal prints, and one-of-a-kind-lamps. Today the products and designs from around the world are more accessible, so creating an exotic bedroom is easy. All you need is a sense of adventure.

For example, African drums create unique nightstands and accent table. Asian temple doors make wonderful room separators and headboards. Beaded shawls and embroidered textiles fabricate fascinating pillows, draperies, and table runners. Tribal rugs make head-turning blankets. Liberally display pieces gathered from travels. Each item has the power to add significantly to the room's uniqueness.

For example, the Moroccan theme flourishes with rich spicy colors, a harem of decorative pillows, and metallic accents throughout. Many cultures use unique carvings and woodwork to put their own signature of style on distinctive furnishings. Incorporating these pieces into your décor instantly imparts the flavor of the land from which it came.

Creating Your Rich Looking Bedroom

In many richly styled bedrooms, glowing wood and polished stone floors play host extravagantly patterned rugs. The inspirations for richly styled bedroom are plentiful and can reflect Italian, Spanish, or French influences, as well as many others.

A romantic at heart, this Old world space is timeless refuge from modern-day living. The style should be indulgent, opulent, and timeless. Walls should be softly tinted, deeply glazed, or ornately papered. Shapely furnishings boast ornate carvings, gentle curves, and distressed unmatched finishes.

Chose copious amounts of fabric-rich velvets, brocades, silks-spill from grand canopies and rods, putting luxury on the floor.

The bed should be the throne of the room. The bedding ensemble is embellished with elaborate trims, tassels, and braids. Accessories embody the charm of the ages and include crystal vases, marble busts, treasured artifacts, and heirloom collectibles. The details of an expressive style are truly personal.

Finishes of wood and metal are often unmatched and distressed to impart age and character to the room, others contrast with touches of gold and hand-painted detailing

The lighting must be seductive; the bedside lamp is just one of many lighting options. Shapely sconces, an elegant chandelier, and hidden up lights are ideal ways to illuminate and enhance the room's ambience. Accessories abound treasured photos in silver frame, European oil paintings, leather-bound books, and elegant vases filled with flowers that speak the language of romance Excess in details becomes the hallmark of this richly appointed room.

Creating Your Passion Boudoir

French women are famous for creating the sexiest bedrooms in the world, and like many French women, today's homemakers often plan for sex and decorate creating evocative, enticing bedrooms. Here are a few suggestions for creating a Passion Boudoir:

Flattering colors contribute to personal beauty and are erotically appealing. Choose seductive colors like rouge red, lipstick reds, creamy peaches, and subtle pinks. Make sure the colors enhance your natural beauty. Be daring and use bold colors on the walls.

Luscious fabrics will set the stage for pampering times. Use silky, velvet, and chenille textures in combination with fluff textures. Use fabrics that remind you of a favorite-shared memory. Exotic patterns, such as animal prints or tropical florals, conjure images of faraway journeys.

Placing mirrors in unusual places, such as the tops of dressers or side tables, reflect dancing candlelight. Tropical plants and trees, uplit with special lights, also cast exciting shadows. An intimate bistro table, set with two chairs, invites private conversations. Dressing tables, furnished with feminine accessories and intimate objects, add mystery and romance to a room. The presence of a bed tray suggests the possibility of the ultimate pleasure: breakfast in bed, while soft lighting, candles, essential oils in a diffuser, and gentle oscillating fans effectively complete the décor in a Passion Boudoir.

Creating Your Reading Room

Even though we think of the bedroom as a pampered place some women don't. If you're one of the many people who love to read in their bedrooms, you might consider designing your bedroom with lounging and reading books in mind.

Since eye experts warn that it's bad for a person's eyes to read while lying down (because we tend to hold the book too close), you might begin by enabling proper reading posture by installing padded headboards.

Another consideration is lighting. Eye experts claim that readers need at least two reading lamps of at least 175-200 watts, but that type of lighting would seem quite harsh in a bedroom setting.

Many feel that their reading time is some of my most important time, intellectually, spiritually, and emotionally. It's the most intimate time I give myself; it compares to what others may call meditation. Just being in a space that's warm and comfortable with a good book is the greatest thing in the world to me, and any bright light would change the ambience of that quiet time." Consider equalizing the overall lighting scheme by adding other less obtrusive lights across the room.

Good colors for Reading Rooms include Old World Ivory, Antique Amber, Sage Green, and Slate Blue. These soft colors reflect light without glare and also support peaceful feelings.

Squishy pillows, luxurious Afghans or throws, landscape paintings with distant horizons, and mirrors for private reflections add feelings of indulgence. A great lounge chair with a floor lamp and nearby tea table completes the additions to a perfect Reading Room.

Creating Your Private Sanctuary

Perhaps you'd rather turn your bedroom into a personal retreat, where you can escape and unwind from a busy day. Surround yourself with photos of friends, family, and places you love, as well as your favorite artwork and meaningful mementos. Under-furnished private sanctuaries can also give you the space to contemplate and daydream.

Good colors for private sanctuaries include dark Forest Greens, deep Chocolates, Mochas, Navy or Cobalt Blues, and Eggplant. Darker colors create a womb-like feeling and aid in getting into a deep sleep.

A small refrigerator will make you feel as if you can enjoy your time in the bedroom without interruption, and a television offers the opportunity to watch your favorite movies and shows. Room-darkening window coverings also encourage deep sleep and aid in the restoration of your soul.

Finding the Best Bedroom Colors

Paint the room with rambunctious color. The best bedroom colors are found in the skin tones of all races, pearly beiges and tans, creamy cocoas, blushing pinks and peaches, subtle yellows, pale violets, and earthy reds.

There are a wide variety of warm pastel colors, as well as more pigmented rich tone such as coral, chocolate, butter cream, terra-cotta, cinnabar, raspberry, aborigine, burgundy, copper, gold and bronze. Pure white, gray, black, blues, and gray greens can create a gorgeous look, but when they dominate, they make the room too chilly to be sensual.

If your bedroom is decorated in cool colors, bring in complementary warm tones. This can be done in many ways: a new coat of paint, sheets, lamp, pillows, throws, art, comforters, slipcover, rugs, tablecloths, flowers, candles, vases, etc…

Creating Your Pleasure Zone

Here are a few simple things you can do to make your bedroom a pleasure zone that you and your partner will enjoy.

- ❖ Paint the walls a warm inviting color.
- ❖ Purchase nightstands and lamps if you don't have any.
- ❖ Place a few exotic photos, prints, books and pampered statuettes in strategic locations.
- ❖ Place several exotic plants in your bedroom. Use some of the petals from the flowers to decorate your bed and enhance the room from time to time.

- ❖ Bring a fur rug or huge soft and fluffy throw into your bedroom.

- ❖ Include fabrics that will invite touching and feelings of comfort. Fabrics that feel like smooth silk, soft cotton, silky satin, rich velvet, overstuffed pillows, cozy comforters, and fluffy bedspreads are most inviting.

- ❖ Scatter pleasant scents around the room. Scents that are fresh and clean are the best smells, Placing scents that your partner likes around the room will remind him of you when he smells those scents again.

- ❖ Keep chilled wine or his favorite drink on hand. It's great for sipping before, during and after intimate moments.

- ❖ Have a picnic in bed. Include finger foods and be sure to have plenty of fresh fruits and vegetables. The things you like in bed should be a part of your "List of things to bring." Don't forget the napkins.

- ❖ Place soothing colored lights in various outlets. Red, or pink lights are great! To help things get going, dance in the dimmed lights for him.

- ❖ Candles are great illuminators for soft lighting. Scented candles are even better. The flickering of the candlelight can help lovemaking become more exciting.

- ❖ Make sure the bed linens are clean, fresh and a pleasure to lie upon. Lots of pillows and soft, plush blankets are highly recommended.

- ❖ Place a props and supplies box beside your bed. Keep your games, body oils, scents, clean towels, tissues, erotic literature and other props here.

- ❖ Find out what colors he likes and have touches of his favorite colors on hand. Have his favorite music available. If he's crazy about jazz be sure to have it. If he likes peanut butter, have some for him. Whatever he likes - be sure to have it. Stock up, let the passion flow and work on becoming the best lover you can be.

- ❖ Light a candle before intimacy and tell your lover he can do anything he likes to you - while the candles are lit.

- ❖ Live in the moment. Keep your mind, body and spirit where you are - with the person you're with.

When asked, "What do you like to take to bed?"
Barbara Streistand stated, on the Oprah Winfrey show....
"I like to take my favorite things to bed."

16

Creating a Comfortable Bathing Space in Your Home

This chapter will help you create the ultimate retreat; a luxurious, bathing space with an appealing style of your own.

The bathroom is the ultimate retreat, the space where, even in a busy home, you should be able to find peace and privacy. You can indulge in a candlelit soak, or enjoy an hour of spa inspired treatments. The room where we bathe and refresh should be practical and functional. But like any area of you home, it's the personal details that make it truly comfortable. Furnished with style, a bathing space can be sumptuous and unique. Your entire home and especially your pampering area can be an endless source of inspiration. The style should be easy, carefree and fun. It should also be an expression of you, your family and your lifestyle.

Your Style

There's often a divide between the bath of your pampering dreams and the reality of your own bathroom, but it doesn't have to stay that way. With a little imagination and a few creative basics, you can achieve a new look more easily than you might think. The first step in getting the kind of bath that pampers - the bathroom of your dreams is learning to understand the best ways to create a comfortable and stylish pleasure zone.

Because bathroom styles evolve the space works if it suits its users; if it's comfortable and if it pleases the senses. Follow the lead of what you like and begin your project by gathering a collection of style ideas that appeal to you from books and magazines. Look at colors and textures that will make you feel good in your bathroom space. Choose patterns that emphasize in the smaller spaces of the bathroom. Think in terms of wet and dry when selecting textures, and take into account how they'll react to the moist environment of a bathroom.

Your Bathroom Layout

The layout of the bathroom should bring a soothing feeling to mind. It is defined by the tub, shower, sink, toilet, and built in storage. Although not impossible to replace, these are the more challenging items to change.

New colors or a fresh crop of textures, however, can also alter the feelings of the space. Bringing in some furniture - a simple upholstered chair or a low bench will add comfort. A quick change to the quality of the room's light, accomplished through new window treatments, mirrors, bulbs or the light fixtures themselves, can completely transform the atmosphere of the bathroom.

Be creative with your choices and keep in mind that it doesn't take much to make dramatic changes in the bathroom. Even the smallest details in that space can go a long way in pampering.

A Simply Perfect Bathroom

The simplest pampering pleasures are often the most satisfying, especially in the bath. The sweeping clean fixtures, white towels, well placed windows, the perfect shade of periwinkle blue illustrates that 'less is more.' The uncomplicated bath easily integrates fixtures, finishes and accent with style.

There are probably as many ideas of what constitutes a well-styled bathroom as there are people who use them. Start with the basics. The size and shape of each space often suggests a particular style of décor. Start with clean finishes, lots of white and pleasing accents, and build from there by adding accessories to the room over time.

Your Bathroom Furnishings

Like any other area of your home, a bath welcomes fine furnishings. A furnished bathroom is a place where you can close the door on the world and relax. Ideally, we'd all love to have a bathroom that has soft places to sit and lounge, to daydream, to sip a cup of tea. Even if you don't have that much space, you will need surfaces for setting drinks and books, and storing, and displaying all of those beautiful little items that are a part of grooming that help satisfy the senses.

It doesn't take much to make a bathroom special. Adding a few simple pieces can make it more comfortable. A vanity stool upholstered in terry cloth, a side table for books or topped with candles, lotions and bath salts, even a spare dining chair piled high with clean towels can transform a space. Free standing furniture offers amenities equal to built ins and it makes a space feel more pleasurable.

If you have the luxury of doing more, choose furniture that invites lounging. Sofas, comfortable chairs and chase lounges are wonderful additions to a bathroom. They customize your space and add character. Bring in the style of pieces you've used in other areas of the house, especially if you like views through doorways to reveal a spirit of consistency and décor.

Try arranging your bathroom furniture to define zones: wet and dry, for example, or different areas for kids and parents. Begin if possible by working parts of your bath (those areas where you probably want privacy such as the toilet, the tub and the shower) from the areas you plan to use as a spa or dressing room. Then, think in terms of style, comfort, care and pampering.

When choosing bath fabrics, look for materials that are absorbent, stain resistant, easy to maintain in humidity, and long wearing. Chenille and terry cloth for example, look stylish on seating and, just like your favorite bathrobe, they feel wonderfully luxurious against the skin.

A furnished bath offers escape and a break from the stresses of the day. Furnishing can make a bathroom a peaceful retreat as well as an attractive bathing space.

Your Bathroom As A Pampering Spa

What could be better than a rejuvenating soaking space that shares the best features of bath, lounge, and spa? Adding comfortable amenities to a bathroom brings elements of the spa experience home, and makes the bath a luxurious and inviting in-home destination.

For domestic bliss there's nothing quite like a bath fitted out as a spa. Most of us tend to think of our baths as a functional space, meant only for private use. Instead try thinking of it as a room for living and relaxing and possibly for sharing conversation with a family member or a close friend. In Japan the tradition of enjoy communal soaks in deep, steaming tubs has been practiced for centuries. Today, home baths are growing larger and more luxurious as more people strive to bring the delights of the spa experience into their daily lives.

Ideally, place a spa space in a separate room, away from areas where more privacy is preferred. Make your tub a focal point in the room - the area that people can use together or individually - and construct a spa environment around it. The spa can be a whirlpool bath, hot tub, or large-scale bathtub. In addition, seating - a built - in bench along the window, perhaps, or a chaise lounge tucked in the corner makes the bath a comfortable gathering place.

For sheer sensual gratification a pampering bath offers numerous possibilities. For example there's nothing like the unexpected pleasure of finding smooth wood and soft pillows in a room where chrome and cool tile are the norm. Imagine the luxury of a terry-upholstered chaise, inviting you to stretch out with a favorite book after bathing.

Take the opportunity to surround yourself with an array of textures. Accessorize with sponges, smooth stones and tropical plants. Bring in a woven rug for stimulating texture under bare feet, or a polished wood table for a surface that's smooth to touch. Revel in the harmony of natural materials and soothing water.

Make your bath a haven. Whenever possible, splurge on soft textures, scrumptious furnishings, and little details that make you feel relaxed. Think of an especially memorable visit to a spa or a well-appointed hotel, and try to recreate the aspects of that environment that you found so relaxing. Bring in aromatherapy candles, piles of especially fluffy towels, or a tub side tray to hold a cup of tea. The details that linger are most always simple and sublime.

17

Tricks of the Trade
That Bring Pleasure

There is no right or wrong way, only the way that's right for you.

D o something to make yourself feel better about how you look. Here are some sure fire tips that you can use to pamper yourself.

1. Visiting a nail spa or painting your fingernails a pretty color. Tweeze your eyebrows. Get a facial or do one at home.

2. For oily skin an oatmeal mask will do wonders. It draws the oil out of your pores. Oatmeal is soothing to your skin as is evidenced by all the lotions that contain oatmeal.

3. Keep some bath salts or bubble bath around your home so that you can soak in a hot bath. A hot bath is very relaxing by itself and with your lover. If you really want to help your muscles try an Epson salt bath. Epson salt is great for pulled, sore and bruised

muscles. It's especially nice if you have been carrying a lot of heavy items. Add a few candles, turn off the lights, lean your head back against a bath pillow and relax. Allow your mind to drift.

4. Take a yoga class. Yoga is one of the best ways to relieve stress. You'll learn how to breathe when you become stressed so that you can minimize the effects of stress as they happen.

5. Buy yourself flowers. Flowers are an inexpensive way to pamper. Have a vase of them at home and on your desk at work. They will cheer you up when you are feeling overwhelmed and are a good reminder to breathe and relax.

6. Light scented candles in your home. Candles are inexpensive and there is no reason you cannot use them every day. Lavender is a very relaxing and soothing scent which can be especially helpful after a rough day

7. Regularly schedule time just for you. If you have children, trade off with another mom and watch her kids on the day that she wants to spend time to herself.

8. Spend time doing what you really want to do without any distractions. Go shopping or catch a movie matinee.

9. Keep a gratitude journal. Remind yourself of *all* that you already have. A journal really does help when you are feeling stressed or overwhelmed!

Contrary to what we tell ourselves making time to pamper yourself can actually give you more time to do the things you need to do because you will be less stressed, and more able to handle your life.

When I get a `little money I find a way to pamper myself;
if any is left, I buy food and clothes.

18

Experience 'Me-Time'

In this chapter you will experience more than 100 Me-Time Rituals that you can incorporate into your lifestyle of pampering.

Today you're going to understand why spending small amounts of quality time on pampering are important to your inner pleasures.

At some point this week you need to schedule time to do something that you love while alone. Take a walk, have a long luxurious shower or bath, read a favorite book, work on a scrapbook, eat your favorite dessert, complete a sewing project, or watch a movie. It does not matter what you do with your 'me-time' just as long as you take time to treat yourself special. It's all about YOU!

A true diva loves her self and attends to her needs in more ways than one. She'll spend at least an hour or more each day taking care of herself. Taking time to feel pampered, petted, stroked and cared for is easier than most people think.

When you finally start loving yourself, don't worry; you are not being selfish; you deserve all of it! Listed below are over 150 pampering treats. Many women contributed to this chapter and gave their version of what 'me-time' means to them. As you read you'll notice they are similar, yet very different in their approach and fulfillment. Read, enjoy and indulge in them in your own ways.

Become a Diva

1. **Be a Diva for a day**. Avoid any effort or stress. Stay in bed; take frequent naps, baths, and pampering moments. If you decide to get out of bed stay in your pajamas. Have food delivered, drink herbal tea and relax. Do only what you want and what you like during your Diva moments.

2. **Create rituals that make you feel pampered and cared for.** Stop to take in life's wonderful beauty and the experiences that make your life more enjoyable. Indulge in the kind of rituals that make you feel like your life is worthwhile.

    My friend Carol sets aside an hour each day to do something for herself. She gets out her best bath oils and takes a long soothing bath without interruption. Another friend, Marva, sips wine from time to time and relaxes by watching a movie.

    Why not develop your own me-time rituals that will help you unwind or relax after a long day. What rituals can you develop for yourself?

Connect With Friends

3. **Make a date with your best girlfriend** for tea at the nicest and trendiest restaurant in town. Dress up, put on your favorite heels and have the valet park your car. Don't deny yourself. Enjoy wonderful little pastries with a warm cup of your favorite tea.

4. **Spend time with your friends.** Take the time to do wonderful and healthy things with your friends. Be sure to include plenty of body, mind and soul retreats.

5. **Invite friends over just to eat.** Ask friends to come over and eat together. Have a few delicious bite size snacks and wonderful drinks available for them. Talk, laugh and do nothing for at least four hours. Have lots of fun.

6. **Have weekly girls' group times**. Meet as a group; go out to dinner, tell wonderful stories and share each other's favorite wines.

7. **Give a signature gift that pampers.** I usually give bottles of wines or wonderful perfumed soaps. Jackie O always gave large uncut semi-precious stones that people could use as paperweights. You can show up with a box of stationary with gold embossed initials (beautiful and cheap at Hallmark). Some people give fresh baked bread, candles, linen, leather journals, or other meaningful items. What would you give as your signature piece? Decide what it would be, then do it

Make Your Home a Haven

8. **Clean your house.** Tell yourself over and over that I deserve a clean house, a made bed, clean clothes, etc. I tell myself that I'm doing these things for me and cleaning up after everyone is a blessing for them. Instead of being angry at how much mess my family can produce it actually motivates me to keep moving!

9. **Put everything in its place.** This is not a way to find perfection, but it is a way to find mental peace. One of the most pampered feelings in the world is to sit in the midst of a clean home. A home that has a sense of neatness and organization is the best way to celebrate your home. It's easier to feel glamour when you're surrounded by cleanliness. Having moments that you feel your home is in order and under control instead of 'under construction' is a luxury within itself.

10. **Make your home a haven for your olfactory senses** (smell) with the most wonderful aromas. Some of my suggestions are: baked cookies, mulled apple cider, burning your favorite incense, dabbing essential oils onto light bulbs, misting rosewater into the air and placing beautiful flowers in every room.

11. **Love yourself at home.** Spend time at home. Sit sometimes and look around finding reasons to feel blessed at how far you've come and how much you've achieved. Every Saturday, no matter what you "should" be doing, make sure you pamper your home by cleaning or doing something special to it.

12.   **Indulge in a bathroom makeover.** Fresh flowers and scented candles go a long way here. A beautiful hamper, matching towels and decorative soaps adds much in a small space. Change the lighting for ambience and dramatic effects. Your wallpaper can also add to the personality of your bathroom. My pharmacist's bathroom used outdated-old prescriptions on his bathroom wall as wallpaper. It was gorgeous! You can also use newspaper from the year you were born, old letters or postcards are great too. Be original and come up with something really great. Add expensive hand towels and your bathroom has a new look and a new life.

13.   **Use fabric softener on your bed linens.** Pamper yourself by using vanilla-lavender scented Downy on your master bedroom sheets and towels. Oh my gosh, it's heavenly. It's a bit more expensive than regular Downy (most times I use generic) but this is my one indulgence.

14.   **Buy high-count (thread) cotton sheets.** Once you try it you'll never go back. The thread count is good when it's 300 and anything above that is better. They're kind of expensive, but worth every dollar. I suggest you hunt the bargain tables at TJ Maxx, Ross, Marshall's, and Tuesday Morning etc. Some of the designer outlet stores are great for finding linen bargains. High-count cotton sheets are the best sheets in the world to sleep under.

15. **Warm your bath towels.** We all know how it feels to encounter the after-chill from a warm shower or bath. Try investing in a towel warmer so that as soon as you step out of the tub you can wrap your body in warmth. If you can't afford a towel warmer, a clothes dryer will do just fine. If you don't have a towel warmer, buy a small radiator looking heater that I bought from Wal-Mart. Leave the towel on it for about ten or fifteen minutes. By the time you get out of the bath; your towel is warm and ready.. You can find portable towel warmers at most selected bath stores.

16. **Enhance your bedroom.** I've already talked about the need to be neat and clean, having a place you can call your space somewhere in your home, and creating different kinds of rooms in your home. This is a little reminder that your bedroom should be a place of simple luxuries that make you feel good just thinking about it. It's the kind of luxury you have that's calming, relaxing and fulfilling. The time that you spend in your bedroom should be looked upon as the most valuable time spent in your home. It should reflect who you are and the kind of life you want to live. It should contain the things you love. You can always add to it. The most important thing to do is surround yourself with loving things that make you feel good about being who you are and where you are.

Get On the Road Again

17. **Take a few of your favorite things on the road.** If you travel often, I'm sure you get lonely and miss home sometimes. The best

way to solve this problem is to take familiar objects with you while on the road. What are the things that will make you feel most at home while traveling? What about candles, framed pictures of loved ones, your favorite pillow, a bathrobe, your favorite blanket or bath gels and oils? What about that favorite shirt or sweats? Bring anything things that will make you feel more at home in a place you can't call home.

Visit a Garden

18. **Buy or pick fresh flowers** as often as possible - even just happy carnations or daisies (which last forever) can make everything brighter.

19. **Go for a walk in a flower garden.** This is something that always picks up spirits and can be done with or without spending any money. It's best to do this during spring or summer. Take a walk in a public garden. Two of my favorites are rose gardens; one is part of a public park and the other is part of the grounds at our local College. The scent of fresh flowers fills the air and it's a beautiful place to renew your spirits.

20. **Go to a flower nursery.** The best are the local special nurseries, not the big flower sections of a mega store. Check out all the variety, the color and the scents.

21. **Plant a flowerbox**. Maybe buy a 6 pack of pansies or petunias to brighten a corner, but mainly just experience walking through all this beautiful variety. Flowers remind me that we go through stages too and we aren't always at a beautiful stage. Maybe we're still in bud and not yet ready to display our blossoms, but we will! I don't beat myself up with critical thoughts while I'm there... no mental lecture about stalled gardening projects or anything. Just a time to enjoy the beauty and the variety of life in my own little world.

22. **Go to a public garden.** I am really fortunate, as I have a friend who lives in Pasadena, CA. and there's three lovely gardens' nearby. I can walk to the Huntington Gardens and Library. I can also drive 8 minutes to reach the Los Angeles County Arboretum (to the East) or the Descanso Gardens (to my West.) I love my own gardens at home, but they are small. It seems that nothing picks me up like a stroll in a really BIG garden. There are so many varieties of plants, trees, flowers to see - I find that being in Nature's bounty heals my soul and mind. I can quiet down and just enjoy lovely blossoms and listen to the birds sing. Yesterday I went to the Huntington and spent nearly an hour in the cactus conservatory, glorying in spiky, knobby, and furry plants. My brother gave me a plant from there a number of years ago as a Mother's Day present. While this shocked me that he was thinking of me, it was perfect for me. I look at it every day and my heart is reminded of him. The plant is healthy and strong, just as he is. Best of all, I put in about 4,000 steps by visiting garden. I tend to walk about and enjoy Mother Nature's bounty. Who could ask for anything more.

Reading Time

23. **Visit a bookstore.** I visit a bookstore and then I buy a really decadent coffee or tea drink. I wander around reading pieces and parts of books. I top the visit off by going to the music section, putting on headphones and listening to the latest releases of my favorite artists. All for the cost of that delicious drink...about $3!

24. **Read a good book while pampering.** Reading! I can't even remember the last time "I" got to read a book of my own. So, after getting some routines in place I'm now left with lots of time to read my new mystery books. By noontime, my morning routines are already done. At night, I apply my facial mask and set up my foot spa a couple of nights a week after the kids retire to bed. It's been a while since I've taken care of me, and boy, do I enjoy it!! Thanks to 'me-time', I feel totally pampered.

25. **Find a quiet place to read.** Lately, I've been taking my favorite book and finding a quiet place to read and drink a good cup of coffee. Sometimes I stay at the coffee shop, sometimes I go to the reading room in the library, and sometimes I just sit in the car. What a glorious thing to have a block of time to sit clear-headed and read a book! It rejuvenates my mind and spirit! When I return home I greet my family refreshed and ready to give them my full attention. I highly recommend a little peace and quiet as you indulge in your 'me-time' pampering.

26. **Quietly read.** Mine is so simple, but it took me years to get here. Our house starts very early. I let the frantic carrying on of getting everyone out of the house, and then I sit down with my cup of tea and the newspaper and spend 30 minutes for me before I start my day. I can quietly read, eat, breakfast and enjoy my tea then I'm ready to get on with my morning routine. Those 30 minutes are a wonderful break after the frenzy and I have learned to sit down and enjoy it.

27. **Go to the local bookstore for an hour or two.** I buy a cup of coffee and read all the books and magazines I want. Sometimes I buy something, sometimes not. I find this is better than the library, because the bookstore sells coffee and treats to eat. They always have the newest reading material. The peace and quiet rejuvenates me and I'm a better mom and wife when I get home.

28. **Have some sit down time.** I work four days a week at the town library, and two hours a week teaching knitting. Between those things I fit in the regular things that all moms do; Drs. Appointments, shopping, errands, etc. I can't find a big chunk of time to do any pampering so I try to fit in small ones. I pamper myself with a time to sit down, savor my favorite chocolate bar, read a chapter of the latest book I've bought. I am one that can really immerse myself in my reading, so it's an escape for me no matter how short the moment. I really do appreciate these times.

Go to the Movies

29. **Rent your favorite movie.** I love to rent a beautiful old movie. It brings back memories of my childhood days and the wonderful times I had while growing up. It's the best!

30. **Watching a chick flick** or one of my favorite heroine movies, curled up on the couch doing absolutely nothing else but watching.

31. **Treat yourself to the movies.** I live alone and work full-time plus go to school full-time. I work 9/80's, which means I have every other Friday off. I treat myself to a day at the movies - with popcorn, candy and a drink. It's one of my favorite pastimes. Here, I can truly relax and escape from the day-to-day reality.

A New You

32. **Get an inexpensive new-do.** I love going to our local cosmetology school. The most expensive thing they have is only $15.00, and you can have a wash, cut, style, massage, and manicure - all very relaxing. The students work on you, but the teachers are all there monitoring - no mishaps that I've ever experienced. The particular school that's close to me is part of a junior college so it also has a culinary arts program. I usually stop for some "specialty" coffee and a small treat for very cheap or free.

33.   **Get a new up-do.** Wear your hair up sometimes. Up-do's can make you feel regal and pampered, all at the same time. Your attitude even improves when wearing a new do. A new up-do not only makes you walk with elegance, it exposes your neck and shows your earrings. It also makes you turn your head more elegantly or at least it gives the appearance of elegance with each move of your head. Wear open blouses or button downs so that you won't ruin your new do when it's time to take your clothes off.

Use Essential Oils

34.   **Invest in Olive Oil for pampering.** Between housework and yard work, my hands get abused! A couple of months ago, I happened on this by accident: it was bedtime, I had just washed my rough and chapped hands, and my lotion was missing from the bathroom counter. There was a bottle of pure, cold-pressed olive oil there, as I had been making some aromatherapy goodies, and after I had patted my hands on the towel, leaving them slightly damp, I poured a couple of drops into my palms and rubbed them together, really fast and firmly, until they heated up. Then I massaged the warm oil into my warm hands for only about 30 seconds, and I couldn't believe how my hands soaked it up! They weren't greasy or anything and the quick massage felt wonderful. When I woke up the next morning, my hands were soft and new again! Now, I almost never use lotion - anytime I wash my hands, I just use 1 drop of olive oil while they're still a bit damp, along with a little friction and a mini-massage. It feels great, feeds my skin, repairs

damage, and protects them from housework. It's a wonderful, quick treat at the end of any job. At night, I use a couple of drops, massage for a whole minute, and let sleep take care of the rest of the job.

35.   **Rub on a little oil.** Before I do dishes, I rub some essential oil or my favorite oil-based lotion into my hands and then don rubber gloves. The hot water and rubber help the oil penetrate and soften my hands so I end up with a shiny sink and soft hands!

36.   **Make your own scented body oil.** Ahhhhh, the feeling of luscious skin, the gentle smell of your favorite cologne, but body oils can cost too much to afford. Instead of spending your money on expensive bath and body oils, why not just make your own? Let's face it, the old way of simply pouring baby oil in your bath water just doesn't get you the aura you want. Perfume merely dissipates in hot water, but it binds to oil. Instead of wasting your perfume, here is what you should do: Pour 1/2 cup of baby oil into a bowl, and then add a few drops of your best perfume into the oil. Swish it around for a few seconds then pour some or all of it into your tub. The oil won't evaporate, and it helps hold the perfume scent for you. Add some fresh flower petals for an extra touch of pampering. Before stepping out of your tub, make sure you have non-slip rug on the floor or a tub-side bath towel. We wouldn't want you to slip and fall on your soft butt.

37. **Try some of the magazine scents.** The perfume industry has provided both men and women the opportunity to get free samples for less. Most fashion magazines come with free perfume inserts. From this day forward rip them out and simply rub them on your wrists for a new scent that will last at least three hours. You can put them to work for longer periods of time by placing them in your lingerie drawer, your purse, under a pillow or in your car. It won't be seen, but it will send a powerfully wonderful scent. You can also tuck them away in the bottom of cabinets, washrooms cabinets, trashcans, linen closets, guest room closets and sock drawers. What a wonderful treat for guests.

Take Care of Your Face

38. **Get a "makeover".** Most cosmetic counters will do this for free at major department stores. You can call a cosmetics salesperson or beauty consultant and they will teach you how to take care of your skin.

39. **Get your eyebrows waxed.** It's not as painful as it sounds - honest - and it opens your whole face up when it's done. I like to think of it as my non-surgical facelift secret. Your eyes so perky afterwards.

40. **Baking soda face scrub.** Just a tiny bit can be gently rubbed onto your shower-moistened skin then rinsed off. Your skin will feel brand-new.

41. **Salt scrub**. GENTLY rub on your entire body. Avoid your sensitive areas. Rinse off under a warm shower. Your feet might need a little extra work and a deeper touch. When my skin's extra dry, I mix the salt with a bit of olive oil first. A drop of fragrant bath oil is nice, too.

42. **Exfoliate.** While my husband was away on business I decided to pamper myself after completing my routines. First I laid out my shaving supplies (including a new razor blade) & filled a soaking tub with warm water. Next I used an exfoliating cream on my legs and then I washed them (like I was giving myself a facial on my legs). After the wash, came a warm towel & a detailed shaving. I finished it up with a nice leg massage complete with lotion. Afterward, my legs felt rejuvenated. The next day, I just smiled at myself when I walked into work as I felt my pants rubbing against my freshly shaved, silky legs. When my husband came home, he was blessed; he thought it was all for him (my little secret).

43. **Get a facemask.** I give myself a manicure, pedicure or a deep conditioning hair treatment. I then take a LOOOOONG steamy shower until I am good and pruned. I slather myself with Shea butter or my favorite lotion afterwards.

44. **Pamper your face.** Every Saturday I take a little time out for my favorite pampering. First, I take out a deep conditioning mask for my face that was given to me by my very best girlfriend. When I massage it into my hair and smell the wonderful scent, it makes me

think of my friend and how blessed I am to have her in my life. Then, I treat myself. This consists of sleeping or reading a good book. By the time this routine is done, I feel like a million bucks!

45. **Put your best face forward**. I take five minutes to put on makeup every day. It's just for me. I smile each time I look in the mirror because I know I'm worth it. I show myself a little love by taking time for me. I'm sure my husband appreciates it - not because he believes that makeup makes me look more beautiful (he actually prefers me without it). He knows that I feel like myself and a bit more pulled together because I've taken those five minutes to pamper myself. Other's comment how "fresh" I look. I think it's actually the inner beauty showing through because I took care of myself in a small way that gives me huge smiles and feels like I hugged myself. I hope every woman finds a small way to pamper herself - we're all worth it!

Give Your Nails Proper Attention

46. **No more nail biting**. Anyone can do this, but it means a lot to me since I have bitten my nails most of my 55 years (with a few brief stretches of "sort-of" quitting). I have actually paid for a manicure three times--hey! I will not pick off what I paid good money for - and even got adventuresome enough to let the manicurist put some COLOR on my nails the last two times. I really felt pampered and encouraged that my hands could look so good. No more nail-biting because I'm special.

47. **Hangnail pampering.** For the past couple of years I have had the worst hangnails and my fingernails were always chipping and breaking. About a month ago I bought a tiny little jar of cuticle cream and a little manicure stick (it cost about $6.00) Everyday for 15 minutes I rub it into my nails, push my cuticles back with the little stick. It's a mini manicure everyday and it fits right into one of my sit down for 15 minutes breaks. I usually drink a glass of water or sip tea too. I get back into my routines feeling totally spoiled. How many people do you know that gets a manicure every day? No more painful hangnails.

48. **Hand softening/cuticle remover.** Before bed & while my hands are still moist, I slather balm on them, and then slip on my *hand socks*. This stuff works great even though it doesn't smell too good. The next morning, I wash my hands and then I use cuticle remover to push back my cuticles. If I don't make myself do this on a regular basis, I get hangnails, which makes me feel totally unfeminine and I'm miserable until they heal.

49. **Pamper hands with salt and olive oil.** Once a week while I'm making dinner and waiting for something to cook, I take a few drops of olive oil and a teaspoon of kosher (coarse) salt and rub it into my hands for a few minutes. The salt gets rid of that yucky winter skin and the oil softens my hands. Then I rinse off the salt and enjoy dinner. This is a fabulous salt and oil scrub.

50. **Paint and trim fingernails and toenails.** File any sharp edges. Give fingernails a coat of clear varnish and toes a coat of any lovely color you like. Well I'm not sure if these qualify as "pampering", but these are things that I do because I love myself and I deserve to be treated well. I paint my fingernails even though they will get chipped and broken at work that night. {Prior to 3 months ago, I painted my nails for my Christmas party and that was it for the year}

51. **Get a paraffin manicure and pedicure.** Not only are they great for your skin, but they also help with arthritis and tendonitis relief

52. **The lock-in facial and manicure.** I lock myself in the bathroom with candles and listen to soft music. I run a bubble bath and while the tub is running, I scrub my face and put on a mask and then I soak in the tub. As I soak, I work on my fingernails. This is so worth the time. I come out smelling nice, my skin is soft and glowing and my fingernails look like I haven't been working all day. To see the look on my husband's face and the way he touches my skin, makes it worthwhile.

53. **Moisturize your feet daily.** I pamper my feet every morning, as I get ready to put on my shoes. I sit down and apply moisturizer to my feet, and use a pumice stone to smooth down any rough spots. I started doing this last summer, and my once rough as sandpaper feet are now very soft and smooth.

54. **Mini manicure and pedicure**. I do a little something every day during a 15-minute break. Monday: Mini manicure and pedicure. Tuesday: Hair mask during my weekly home blessing. Wednesday: Facemask or scrub. Thursday: Shave my legs and moisturize them. Friday: Skin exfoliation. Saturday: Long bubble bath. Sunday: Any 'me-time ritual that makes me feel special. I will admit that sometimes the most I have time for is body lotion after my shower but I am trying! Now that I am wearing shoes during the day my feet are in much better shape and I have started putting a foot cream on every night before bed. My husband was so sweet not to ever say anything but he *has* started offering to rub my feet again.

55. **Ingrown toenail care.** I have ingrown toenails so it's a two-fold session. It's keeping my feet happy and healthy and I love my pretty toes. My nail tech loves to do fancy nail art. It's no extra charge and its great advertisement for her. She matches my big toes to whatever she does on my nails. This means a lot to me because I bit my nails until I was 27 years old. Now I reward myself for having nails by getting them pampered. My nail tech plays soft music and she has the vibrating chair and warms up a neck pillow while having my pedicure. I'm in heaven these moments.

56. **Soak your feet in marbles with a bunch of friends.** I recently went to a home spa party where they were showcasing various lotions, baths products, etc. The hostess filled a plastic tub for each person with very warm water, some moisturizing oil, and marbles. You soaked your feet in the tub and rolled them around on the

marbles. Just like a foot massage! There's no reason why we can't do this at home with our own marbles - it's a treat that really feels special.

57. **Share nail care with a best friend.** One day I visited a friend and she got out her nail care kit, polish, and two little bowls filled with water for soaking, a hand towel for each of us, and we sat, talking, and gave ourselves a manicure. Since I usually don't do this, it was lots of fun, and very needed. It only took about 30 minutes, and we looked and felt great!

58. **Take a footbath.** Take a footbath in hot water. You have to sit for the next few moments, unable to move, so prepare yourself. Have a nice fluffy towel handy to dry your feet, clean socks and something to read. Then you're ready to sit back and relax.

59. **Foot Treatment Lotions.** Smooth lavender scented lotion on your feet before you go to bed and in the morning before putting on socks.

60. **Soak feet in hot water** in a pan or in the tub and finish by scrubbing them with a paste of kosher salt and olive oil. It makes a WORLD of difference in how your feet will feet look and feel! It will soften calluses and rough heels.

61. **Exfoliate your feet.** Do this in the evening. It's a good substitute for a bubble bath. Fill a plastic bucket or pan with very warm water

and set it on a folded bath towel on the floor in front of the sofa. Relax, close your eyes, take a few deep, slow breaths, and soak my feet for 5 to 10 minutes. It's a great way to de-stress. Use a jar of scented sugar scrub to exfoliate your feet and calves. After drying your feet apply foot lotion and put on some white cotton socks. It's a very soothing little bath for your feet after a long day on your feet!

62. **Get an inflatable footbath pedicure!** At one time, Avon was selling an inflatable footbath, with some foot scrub. I bought them and when I need a lift, I fill the footbath with warm water, soak and scrub my feet, clip my toenails and put on a little polish. It makes feet feel perky. It's especially nice to do while watching a movie.

63. **Nail attention.** The most pleasing thing you can do for yourself is a personal manicure. If you can't afford to pay someone to do it for me, try doing it yourself. Set aside an hour and really indulge. Use real olive oil to soften your cuticles. Take time to file your nails to a nice shape, exfoliate with cocoa butter and sugar, and put on a nice hand cream. Paint them a pretty color suitable for the season. If you have a little extra time, try a French manicure. Keeping them nice makes you feel very pampered.

Meditate For Relaxation

64. **Meditate in a big chair.** Pamper yourself by cuddling up in a Lazy Boy rocker with a cup of Sleepy Time Tea. You can clear your

mind, relax for about a half hour and do nothing for the entire time you're in the chair.

65. **Have some 'mindless time'.** I teach our daughters at home and always seem to have paper correcting or research to do in connection with it, and between that and taking care of personal finances of the household I really crave some mindless time. I don't like to watch TV or read magazines very much, so what I do sometimes is play an electronic solitaire game (handheld). It engages my mind a little, but mostly it is a game that does not require serious thought. It's something I can do for myself real quick in between times if I'm getting a bit stressed.

66. **Simply sit alone.** As a part of your nightly routine take the time to sit and do nothing. During that time, you can do anything you like while sitting. You should sit for an hour or so and remember you must do nothing that would cause you to stand up. Do anything, as long as you're sitting. I usually knit, but anything would work, as long as it's something you enjoy and is for yourself.

Take Energizing Naps

67. **Take a nap on the porch.** Swing in your hammock. Drift off to sleep. Taking advantage of a beautiful day to enjoy God's creations is such a renewal of the spirit. It will help you feel like you're giving yourself something beautiful.

68. **Take a nap in the middle of the day.** Take a short nap in your own bed. Not to sleep, but just for not being disturbed. My husband wakes me in about an hour. But I'm not really sleeping; I'm enjoying the silence, reading a book or... whatever.

Sleep Just Because

69. **Warm your bed before you get in.** I like to curl up on the floor for 10 minutes. While I'm doing that I put a heating pad on a towel in the bed under my covers so it will be warm when I finally get in.

70. **Sleep In.** I love Saturdays when we don't have any commitments. It's sort of an unspoken rule in our house that on these rare occasions, I'll be doing a little self-pampering. My husband is a morning person and I'm not, so he always wakes up. I roll over, grab his favorite mushy feather pillow like it's a Teddy bear (I like how it smells of him), and I sleep in another 30 minutes or so. I don't sleep in too long, because I don't want to mess up my weekly sleep schedule. But it's still the best sleep I get all week, because I know he's taking care of everything downstairs. There's nothing like stretching out in that big bed all by myself with absolutely no pressure to hurry up and start the day. I treat myself to a long shower while listening to my favorite 80's tunes. I take advantage of the extra time to deep condition my hair and really shave my legs well. (Versus those ankle-ripping quickies I do during the week.) Lastly, I drench myself in moisturizer, dress in something

nice (of course), and sashay down the stairs, transformed into the well-rested, sexy diva my husband fell in love with.

71. **Go to bed EARLY** with a book and a cup of herb tea after a warm shower with your favorite shower gel--no matter what the rest of the household is doing, and no matter what crisis is happening in anybody else's life, client or friend. Sleep is the very best pamper mission. It's an investment in your ability to care for your family and clients. If you don't make the time to do this on a regular basis, you'll use up my reserves before you know it. If you get worn out or lack sleep you don't work at full level when it's time for you to take care of your family. When rested, you're in a better frame of mind and have more energy to do it.

72. **Make scents a part of your bedtime routine.** As part of developing a soothing bedtime routine, try to signal your body that it is time to go to sleep. Rub your hands with a scented hand cream, lotion or moisturizer. It feels nice, and the smell is calming; it's now a sort of trigger for getting sleepy. Burn a scented candle for about twenty minutes, spray your sheets with a light scent or use some scented moisturizer, just before you tuck yourself in.

More Exciting Ways to Pamper Yourself Daily

73. **Have a pamper room.** Create a room where you can be alone to pamper yourself. Kind of like your pampering sanctuary. It's your place to gather your senses undisturbed. Choose to have it in a

garden, quiet and private part of your home, apartment, or maybe a small corner. My friend Carol built herself a sunroom that was joined to her bedroom, where no one was allowed to enter. It was all hers. She filled it with the kind of furniture she wanted, beautiful mirrors, a hot tub, a plug in coffee maker and teakettle with an ample amount of fabulous coffees and teas. It's the perfect place to sit, relax with a good novel and keep the world away.

74. **Mini-lotion pampering**. Splurge and buy several small bottles of lotion. Place one by each sink, by your bed and computer, to remind you that it's time to moisturize your hands. It also keeps them nice and soft in cold weather.

75. **Have a beauty night**. Thursday evenings are my "Beauty Night's". That's my evening to do my nails, or a facial, or a longer bubble bath, sometimes with a glass of wine and lit candle. I do a pedicure and wear foot lotion and socks overnight. I don't do all of the above every Thursday, but I pick and choose depending on my need, desire, and time. I think my Thursday night Beauty Night stemmed from the need to use Vaseline on dry cracked heels and wear socks to bed - those always seemed to come on Thursdays. When is your beauty night?

76. **Have a full night of pampering.** On Sunday afternoons I give my self a manicure, pedicure, clean my wedding ring, and tweeze my eyebrows. I do this right after arranging my outfits that I'm going to wear for the week in my closet. This routine takes less than an hour

to complete, and I feel so great after taking time to do things just for me. The feeling lasts all week since I'm not searching for clothes in the morning. I love the way my wedding ring sparkles.

77. **Have a pamper party.** We just had a pamper party for one of my best friends who is expecting her 3rd baby--it was a small gathering of 7 of the people closest to her. We each brought small tokens for the baby i.e.: pampers, wipes, bibs, blankets, towel etc--but we pampered her with a manicure and pedicure and also pampered ourselves each with a manicure too! It was a fabulous night. We all enjoyed being pampered and soon the baby will too! So to any of you that know of a friend or family expecting a new family addition, they probably need bibs, pampers, wipes etc and its probably adding up to lots of $$. It's a great idea to pamper a friend.

78. **Take some 'me-time.'** I've worked since he was born and he will be five next week. During hunting season my husband hunts whenever he's not working. Needless to say I was home with my son with no break, because by the time he got home it was 9 PM and he went straight to bed. We made a deal that after hunting season I would have an afternoon to myself on Saturdays. This has proven to be a great energy boost. I usually run errands, but this past week I went to Barnes and Noble, had some coffee and read for 4 hours. I had so much energy when I got home that I cleared all of my hotspots without a moment's hesitation. Pampering yourself can be pampering your mind so you don't lose it.

79. **Redeem a pampering gift certificate.** My husband bought me a gift certificate to a local nail salon for a manicure and a pedicure. This is a sweet gift by itself, but it is made sweeter when he offers to watch our three children when I go to redeem my gift certificate. When I get back home, he has them bathed, hair dried and in bed. Then all I need to do is sing them their bedtime songs and settle in with my husband or a new novel.

80. **Home spa pampering.** As a published author, I have very little time for myself. When I do get a bit of time, I love to lock myself in the bathroom for a home-spa treatment. This is when I soak in the bathtub, shave thoroughly, give myself a facial masque, a pedicure, a manicure, use my pretty scented lotion, etc. I have all these things in my bathroom already, so it's all-FREE! The best part about this is that when I'm done, I feel so pretty and feminine! A variation on this for family fun time is to include my daughter. There isn't a little girl out there who doesn't love a little home-spa pampering with their mama!

81. **Pamper yourself for a whole week.** Once a week my pampering/beauty routine is as follows: **1)** Dry rasp my heels and soles (sometimes at this point I put on hair deep conditioner. **2)** Short or long soak in the tub with bubble bath depending on how much time I have. **3)** Shave legs and underarms (of course I also do this one or two more times during the week too. **4)** Use a nail pumice stick on my fingernails and toenails. **5)** Use pumice on the

159

bottoms of my feet to remove calluses. **6)** Scrub my body with bath gel wearing those scratchy woven gloves. **7)** Rinse off and get out. **8)** Apply tooth-whitening gel for 3-5 minutes. **9)** At the same time apply masque to my face, neck and chest for 10-15 minutes. **10)** In the meantime apply lotion to the rest of my body. **11)** File fingernails and trim and file toenails if necessary (you can put 1-2 coats of polish on your nails too). **12)** Rinse teeth and face and apply face cream. All this only takes 1/2 hour and you feel like a new woman afterward.

I make sure to lock my bedroom door beforehand, and since my bathroom is inside my bedroom if I have extra time waiting for my masque to dry I can do some bathroom and/or room cleanup. I don't think 1/2 hour once a week is too much to spend on yourself. You couldn't drive to the salon and back in that amount of time! Also, there is no law about when you could treat yourself. If you're only free time is in the morning when the kids are at school, by all means do it then.

82. **Enjoy pamper-time while running errands.** Last Saturday morning, I decided to get some errands out of the way - a couple of them were fun errands just for me. I told my husband I was headed out for errands and should be back around lunchtime. I left him with the 2 little ones and off I went. I had such a good time! I went to a fabric store to browse and plan for a new color scheme in the dining room. I didn't spend a dime - I wasn't rushed, didn't have anyone tapping their foot at me, and I dreamed about my next project at home. I stopped by a local bakery and got a little bag of

cookies for the girls. I went to a new scrapbook store to browse. All places I've been meaning to go, but never get a chance to with the little ones. I came home so refreshed, so energized! I've still got a little bounce in my step when I think about how much fun I had. I hope to make this a regular event - perhaps once a month. Just a morning out for ME. Anywhere I want to go! Anything I want to look at! Maybe that's not pampering like a manicure, but I certainly FELT pampered.

Indulge In Relaxing Massages

83. **Hire a massage therapist.** Have a massage therapist come over and give you a full body massage. It's very relaxing. I do this about every two weeks. It is my little way of loving myself so that I can get back to loving my family.

84. **Get a discount massage.** Look for a massage school - students take their time and give great massages for just a fraction of the cost.

85. **Get a full body massage.** I have a full body massage mat that my husband got me for Christmas. I also have a foot massager (you know, the water kind) that he got me 2 yrs ago. Put the two together, add some candle light with some soft music ... Mmmm I'm relaxed already!

Capture the Essence of Bathing

86. **Take a nightly soak**. Since I live alone now, I am free to pamper myself even more. I wouldn't miss my nightly soak with good-smelling salts and such, using fragrant candles whenever I wish, and spritzing the house with fragrant oils regularly.

87. **Have a very hot bubble bath** to ease weary bones. (Used to be my PMS treatment only) Afterwards, I try to put cream on my feet because it helps to prevent work boot feet!

88. **Mix Calgon Bath Oil Crystals and Epsom Salt.** You can buy both at the Dollar Store. It is great for sore muscles and the bath oil crystals make your skin smell good and become softened. You use about a handful each time. One year I put this mixture in inexpensive jars, with a decorative ribbon, and gave them as Christmas Gifts. Everyone raved about how good it made them feel.

89. **Take a nightly shower** about half an hour earlier. Snuggle into a comfy robe, turn back the bedcovers, switch on the night side lamp, and read another chapter of the novel that you checked out from the library. You'll love the quiet peacefulness of your "alone" time.

90. **Take a baby shampoo bubble bath**... if you have sensitive skin. It makes great bubbles too. Light some candles, put on some nice music, turn out the lights, sip some champagne and relax in all those bubbles.

91. **Take a quickie bubble bath.** During the week, take a nightly bubble bath. It's a pretty quick fix. On Saturdays try to get a facial, leave-in conditioner, body scrubs, really thorough leg shaving, and a good book. Before reading my book I usually take a bath. I make sure to do it early in the daytime, since taking care of ME is just as important as almost any other chore on my list.

92. **Take an essential oil bath.** Run a hot bath and add some essential oils to smell up the room. Lemon oil smells heavenly! Apply a mask; the clay or the peel off kind is easy to use/ Soak in the hot, smelly-good tub while it dries and then I take it off. Get out and follow up with a rub down of your favorite lotion. You'll feel so wonderful after that. Use any of your favorite lotions, and then top it off with a facial scrub or foot scrub. Then lie on the couch with a very good book. You know the kind that gets you all teary-eyed?

93. **Take a shower** instead of a luxurious bath. Try taking an entire evening to yourself and have a long lasting pampering shower. An added bonus for me is that it is virtually free.

Enjoy A at Home Spa

94. **Give yourself a "spa".** Take a long bath with oatmeal with a masque on your face and conditioner in your hair; scrub my feet as above; slather on a really good smelling lotion; and really take time to dry my hair.

95. **Have a spa night.** Pamper the whole family and have a "Spa Night." Your whole family will love it. All we do is go to the store (Target, Wal-Mart, whatever) and buy those $1 Facial packets in whatever type you want or need for your skin, and a hot oil treatment for everyone's hair. Spend the evening giving each other facials, massages, and hot oil treatments. Everyone will feel pampered. Take lots of fun photos with towels on everyone's heads and green or pink goop on their faces, lots of laughs and family time together, all for less than ten bucks.

96. **Take time out in a sauna.** Take personal time in a sauna! Hang out for 20 minutes or so. Take a long shower with yummy aromatherapy products. It's very relaxing.

Enjoy Your Favorite Drink

97. **Drink liquid diamonds (aka champagne.)** Drink it to celebrate you. Champagne is so widely accepted that you can drink it before your meal and no one will think it's out of order for you to do so. To bewilder your friends order a glass of French Champagne. Simply ask for Dom Perignon, Bollinger or maybe Cristal. Drinking liquid diamonds is a way to celebrate any occasion.

98. **Take a whole weekend and stay in a hotel** so that you can do lots of girlie things. Go to the museum for a jazz brunch. Drink a mimosa. Swim in the hotel pool. Walk in the park. Get a manicure and/or massage, and eat Chinese food. See a chic-flick. Stop in my

favorite bookshop, and read to your heart's content, with no interruptions. Soak in the hotel tub, and sleep through the night. In short, do whatever you want for a whole day or so, with no guilt, no interruptions! And then come back renewed, and less frazzled.

99. **Replace chipped stemware.** If they are outdated, mix matched or ugly put them in the back of the cabinet or use them as extras. You'll feel more elegant and pampered when you're holding a nice piece of stemware. You can always purchase nice stemware at Ross, Marshall's, Wal-Mart, Kmart or Linens and Things, for a reasonable price. (Under $25.00) You can also visit a local antique store. They usually have lots of sets to choose from. Once you buy your new stemware raise a glass and toast yourself for doing the right thing. Congratulations!!

100. **Name a drink after yourself.** How wonderful is it to have your own favorite drink named after you? It's simple, all you have to do is mix your favorite liquors and then serve it to your friends. Imagine the pampered feeling once your friends catch on to the drink named after you. You can take this further and name a drink or food after a friend.

Drink Your Favorite Coffee, Tea or Cocoa

101. **Treat yourself to a special cup of coffee** and a small treat from a local bakery or coffee shop. Not the chain stores, but those local merchants who really put love and care into what they make

and to whom your business is important. These products are much better tasting and are a real treat to enjoy. I especially like to savor my treat in a quiet spot with or without a good book.

102. **Go groceries shopping** with your friends. It's a great way to relax and get caught up! Sometimes I get a latte when I go grocery shopping. It makes the whole experience better!

103. **Watch a sunrise while enjoying a drink.** Take a cup of tea or coffee onto your front porch and sit in the swing and read a good book or a magazine. Enjoy sitting out there thinking the thoughts that make you happy. Set my timer and don't feel guilty at all!

104. **Drink a good old-fashioned cup of hot chocolate.** Get the flavored kind, but plain chocolate flavor is fine too! At night, get hot chocolate and a can of whipped cream and keep the can with you to put more in as it dissolves!! ~YUMMY~

105. **Have a hot cup of cocoa.** Pamper yourself with a hot cup of either toffee or French vanilla cappuccino topped with whipped cream and a sprinkle of nutmeg. Take a few moments to enjoy this in a quiet spot somewhere -- sometimes even in a nice, warm, bubble bath.

106. **Choose tea over coffee sometimes.** Tea is considered the casual drink of luxury. It was always served in elegant hotels as an alternative to alcohol and coffee. You are usually given a wide

range of teas to choose from. Often accompanied with little sandwiches, pastries, or a variety of scones. The most famous hotels include teas in their menu a la carte. Be sure to wear your best attire for your tea drinking moments. You'll love the experience. What a great way to pamper yourself.

107. **Go out on the back porch** wrapped in a blanket with hot chocolate or hot tea and look at the stars.

108. **Buy a special drinking mug.** Go shopping for a mug of your choice. Find one that will help remind you that you love yourself.

Eat Your Favorite Foods

109. **Learn to cook your favorite meals.** If you have to leave home just to get your favorite meal, you might want to reconsider whether you should learn to prepare it for yourself. Half the fun is finding out that you can do it better. Master the secret of your secret recipe and you'll be smiling from ear to ear as you eat it.

110. **Sip on warm soup.** Simmer two quarts of plain broth from vegetables (no meat or flavorings), and set the hot quarts in Mason jars beside the bed (in a big punch bowl so you don't knock them over). During evening routine or waking up during the night, it's so soothing to sip on them. Then in the morning the leftover broth can be heated up to start the day. For some reason, it's uncomfortable to drink plain room-temperature water,

especially in winter; but heated with vegetables and some warming ginger makes it taste really good.

111. **Enjoy a gentle treat.** Hold up at a dessert or bread shop with your journal, then enjoy a little treat while you write or watch people. Take along a girlfriend for some good chat time. Hope those are inspiring for someone - I know they nurture me!!

112. **Enjoy chocolate.** Taste chocolate in a way that you can embellish it and lavish it for moments of ecstasy. You decide what kind of chocolate treat you will have. Let your tongue linger over the taste. Lick the spoon, lick your fingers, and lick the pot if it makes you feel good. No one has to see you do it. Use the most expensive chocolate you can find. It's a needed indulgence for every soul.

113. **Get a really good chocolate bar or "bon bon"** and take about 5 minutes to eat it with your eyes closed so you can really taste it.

114. **Have any one of your dinners catered** to your home for two, served & cleaned up by the caterers usually for about $50. Special bottles of wine of course add to the expense, but what could be more romantic than staying home, sharing a wonderful meal. Money well spent and well worth it I think!

115. **Take a "Reese's vacation".** Do this anywhere and it costs about 50 cents! Sit somewhere, close your eyes, eat your Reese's (very

slowly), and do all you can to relax and imagine yourself elsewhere. Visualize you're in the Caribbean; climbing the Pitons in Dominican Republic, etc. Imagine the warmth of the sun on your skin, the feel of the sand if there is any, a slight warm breeze, and birds singing. After the Reese's is gone you'll be incredibly relaxed and can handle most anything.

116. **Buy your favorite ice cream**. To pamper yourself buy your favorite ice cream bars. Then have one and curl up with a good book. Spend some quiet time reading and enjoying your ice cream. This is time that you carve out for yourself.

Learn Something New

117. **Ask questions and listen to new ideas.** Once, while at the mall I walked into a specialty popcorn store and asked how they made all that yummy stuff. The lady was alone - she had time - and she loved answering my questions. She showed me how the popcorn was added to a huge kettle, seasoned with specialty toppings, packaged, and prepared for purchase. The popcorn smelled wonderful! I learned something new and sampled a fresh new flavor. It took all of 5-10 minutes, and both the shop employee and I enjoyed ourselves.

Listen To Your Kind of Music

118. **Listen to your favorite music.** When I'm in my car alone and when I'm running errands or going to lunch on this day, I love to listen to relaxing classical music. It really helps me feel like this is MY time and reminds me to do the things I want to do.

119. **Create a theme song you can call your own.** Play it throughout the day to keep you motivated. Listen to it at night. Hear it in your head as you enter a room full of people. Make a tape of it, play it in your car. Use it to float through life at your own speed in your own way. You might choose to select more than one theme song; one that you listen to while with your lover and another that you listen to while at work, maybe even a third when you spend time with family members. You make the choice on what you choose.

Reward Yourself

120. **Get involved in things that lend you applause.** Get involved in community projects, social events or group events that allow people to honestly applaud your achievements. Join your local toastmasters organization to find out about joining organizations and speakers bureaus.

121. **Buy yourself a little treasure.** Some pretty stationery, a scented candle, bath salts, a new lipstick, and some English tea. Now, enjoy them.

122. **Gaze at the stars**. With children your pampering moments are usually inexpensive and short but always needed. Try to always take time to look beyond where you are. Sometimes looking at the stars will give you a whole new perspective.

123. **Watch the sunset.** When I lived in California, I'd savored the sun at the beach. Here in Texas I take it in by a lake near our house.

124. **Write in your journal.** Take out a fresh piece of paper and list every little thing you have achieved in life. Give yourself lots of credit for everything you have done that you felt proud for doing. Be sure to list the smallest and most unnoticed things you've done. Whenever a low moment hits you, pull out your achievement list and let your smile shine through.

Commit To an Exercise Program

125. **Go to a gym before church.** On Sunday mornings before church I go to the gym. There are very few people there on Sundays so I take my time swimming (which I love to do), sitting in the hot tub, the sauna, taking a long shower, taking my time getting dressed before leaving to head home. Sometimes I get coffee on

the way home. There are 5 people waiting at home for me and we only have one full bath so the house is very hectic in the morning. Taking my time at the gym gives me a physical workout and a mental break and I am able to face the week with a better attitude.

126. **Go to the gym and <u>not</u> work out**. I do what I like to call the Pamper triathlon. This is where I take advantage of things in my gym that I feel are extravagant features. First, I hit the whirlpool, then I hit the sauna, then I hit the steam room. I finish up the triathlon as any good athlete does with a long hot shower (the hot water never runs out at the gym). By the time that I am ready to leave I am like a puddle of mush. It feels wonderful and I feel rejuvenated and well taken care of. I know not everyone belongs to a gym and if some do they may not have these features, but for those who do I highly recommend the pamper triathlon. You will feel like a million bucks.

Light Your Own Fire

127. **Light a candle.** I light my favorite candle, put on my favorite CD, kick off my shoes, put my feet up, close my eyes, and totally lose myself in the music for about 30 minutes. Never fails to refresh my spirit and mind.

128. **Build the perfect fire.** Learn to build a wonderful fire and you will never have to beg a man to do it for you. Here's what you

should do: Place two logs across the fireplace with about six inches in between. Twist three or four pieces of newspaper lengthwise and tuck them between the logs, and add a log or two of kindling on top. Light the paper at both ends and snuggle in your most comfortable pajamas in front of a fire you built yourself. Now, curl up with a good book, your favorite drink, some munchies and a soft rug to sit on with lots of cushy pillows scattered about.

Wear Your Beauty with Pride

129. **Wear diamonds, emeralds, pearls, rubies, and jade.** There are so many other jewels that it's difficult to list all of them without my mouth watering. It's easy to be dazzled by these stones, but they're expensiveness can be quite daunting. Don't be afraid, there is one classic piece of jewelry you can buy, wear and afford... pearls! Pearls hold such healing powers that women who wear them are considered Goddesses. A simple pair of pearl studs can add glamour to an otherwise drab face. Elegant pearls are the only piece of jewelry you need to own. You can purchase a nice pearl necklace for about $150.00 at your local jewelry store.

130. **Buy a new pair of pretty silk pajamas and fragrant lotion.** I get all "dolled" up and watch a movie I have rented. I was at my mother's house over this past weekend, and mentioned to her what a fun treat it was and how it made me feel. She told me she

had never done that before! So, we headed out, treated ourselves to new pj's and a movie from our favorite store, (Target) and had a really nice evening together. We didn't spend much money, but it made us feel like a million bucks!

131. **Invest in a beautiful silk scarf.** There are some women who know how to wear scarves and then there are those who don't know how. You can easily transform yourself into one that does. Go to your favorite clothing store, find a beautiful scarf and put it on. Doesn't it feel wonderful? Add a silk scarf to your wardrobe and accessorize your briefcase, a blazer, and a blouse or use it as a belt on a pair of nice jeans. Tie a silk scarf around your neck while driving a convertible and let the wind blow it in the breeze.

132. **Wear a silk robe.** Wear a silk robe around your home for no reason at all. Do the normal things; like washing the dishes, eating breakfast or putting on make-up in your silk robe. If it's long and glamorous answer the door in it. You'll look pampered expensive and well kept to anyone that knocks.

133. **Add a little class to your trash.** Don't be afraid to make a few classy mistakes. Add some trampinees to your wardrobe and mix it with your classiest stuff and watch the fashion statement explode. Many times adding your own ideas will catch on and other women will want to duplicate yours. Add pearls, a pair of high-heels, a silk scarf and the rest you can play by ear. Wear silk underwear and you'll feel like new money.

134. **Spice your underwear.** Placing scents in your lingerie drawer is a great way to add some eroticism to your otherwise dull world. You can try several different scents: rosemary, flower peddles, herbal tea bags, fancy soaps, perfumed sachets, baby powder, small packages of coffee, herbs, incense - anything that sends a great aroma up your nostrils when you open the drawer. Use your own private scent that no one else has to know about. Maybe it's your favorite. The objective is to add a wonderful scented moment to your life every time you open the drawer.

135. **Slip into a pair of your favorite high-heeled backless slippers**. Instant glamour and sex appeal is guaranteed. You will suddenly view the world and all things around it as pampered and precious. High heels can give you that Audrey Hepburn kind of feeling. It's so sexy the way you can cross your legs and dangle one shoe in a sassy manner. Add a pair of sexy heels with a pair of jeans and a favorite sweater and you'll feel sexy all day long. It's just something about wearing a good pair of high-heels.

Be Naughty Sometimes

136. Indulge in a whim or something you've always wanted to do. Go ahead be naughty sometimes. Why not go without panties or try doing something you know your mother would object to you doing. Don't do anything dangerous or ridiculous that might land

you in jail. If you overdo your naughty indulgence it might turn into a bad habit.

Indulge In Pampering Moments Regularly

137. **Have breakfast in bed.** Give your love ones and yourself a little pampering by having breakfast in bed. Just a few things like a cup of tea, bacon and eggs or whatever you like.

138. **Enjoy one of your hobbies.** I use a timer to give myself me-time for my hobbies. It might be drawing, painting, reading, cooking, baking or any other favorite thing. That's all of the moment. I probably have more pamper missions for myself because I have a little money and when there comes a pamper mission which costs me extra money ... I just think about a cheaper replacement.

139. **Swing on the swings at the park.** Bake refrigerated cookies. Watercolor (cheap kids stuff). Have a "tea party" by cutting up Little Debbie's into bite-size pieces and serving tea using the good china.

140. **Check in a nice hotel.** My best friend and I (since 1970) have a girls' night out. We check into a nice hotel near a great shopping center. That night we treat ourselves to a really nice dinner, and the next day we shop 'til we drop. We save our money all year long so we don't go into debt. We have one of these a year, usually around our birthdays in the late summer.

141. **Spend time working on your scrapbooks**. Looking at old scrapbooks or yearbooks. Put on your favorite CD and move to the music or sing along.

142. **Remember wonderful experiences**. I started scrap booking a few months ago and I've found it to be very therapeutic. I've revisited the delicious time in which my husband and I fell in love; different experiences we've shared, the birth of our (now 2 year old) daughter, our wedding, and on and on. While I'm creating the pages I look at the pictures, remember the experience, and re-live that time period while I'm thinking about how I want to portray the experience on paper. It is fantastic, and I come home refreshed with a renewed appreciation for my family, as well as an heirloom that my daughter and husband love to look at! I get pampered and I produce something tangible for my family.

143. **Make a greeting card** by yourself and then write a good message and send it to someone special.

144. **Send a handwritten note to someone you haven't talked to in a while.** You don't need a reason. Notes from good friends are always welcome and enduring. Invest in a box of nice paper with matching envelopes, and don't forget your impression gold-stamped monogram. It's such a wonderful feeling to give and receive a special note from a special friend. From time to time

send yourself a special reminder on your own paper and watch how your heart beats brighter.

145. **Take a family walk.** I like to take a walk with the whole family in the woods or the country. We talk, have fun, and then relax afterwards with a cup of tea at home. That really feels good.

146. **Get rid of the kids one day a week** so I can clean or shop, but mainly just be by myself. Some days all I do is take a nap and read a book!

147. **Enjoy your pets.** No agenda, just petting the cat on my lap or sitting next to one of my two dogs that are too big for my lap, and rubbing a tummy or furry head. They love it, and the extremely simple pleasure puts all worries in perspective.

148. **Stand tall in a crowd.** Standing tall helps you to look like somebody. When standing tall, nice and straight you move through life like a princess. Taking a ballet or yoga class, regardless of your age will make you stand taller. Place a hardback book on top of your head and walk from time to time just to gain a beautiful posture. It really works. Practice, sitting, standing squatting and getting up with the book on your head. Tuck your stomach in, raise your chest to the sky and now you are posture in motion.

149. **Pamper your teeth and gums.** Brush your teeth with toothpaste, floss them, then brush them again with your toothbrush moistened in hydrogen peroxide and then dipped into baking soda. Pay special attention to gently massaging your gums and cleaning your tongue. Rinse thoroughly, being careful not to swallow any. Your mouth will look and feel VERY clean and white.

150. **Draw your life story on canvas.** Think for a moment about what your life has did, done and is doing. Now take those thoughts and put them on canvas. Have your idea of your life placed in a nice frame and hang it where you can see it. Reflect on it from time to time. Create from it your own thoughts, ideas and memories in a way that you can relate to what you were thinking at the time of the drawing. Now take a look at it. Doesn't it look wonderful and it's all yours. It'll be worth more than money to you. Now you can brag on the expensive painting by artist named Ms. You.

151. **Have a picnic.** A pampered woman always has her picnic basket ready to go. At a moment's notice an impromptu occasions are great for picnics. Be sure to include: napkins, blanket, quilt, basket, wine, champagne or both. Pull together some of your other luxuries that you already have - glasses, china, fruit, veggies, appetizers and of course a fabulous dessert. Now pick a place and go on a picnic.

Make People Wonder Who You Are

152. **Rename yourself.** You can step away from your own life for few hours. What do your closest friends call you? If it's different from your own name try using only that name for a whole day. Most authors, celebrities and politicians use a different name when they go to dinner, leaving the ordinary name at home, so why can't you? It only to get rid of the ordinary for a short while. It's exciting and only your best friends can call you by your new and interesting name.

153. **Wear your biggest and darkest pair of sunglasses that you can lay your hands on.** Wear them with pride in the most public place. Sunglasses are the most glamorous way to look expensive. You can buy designer sunglasses from Channel, Prada, and Versace for less than anything else they design. Try pairing your sunglasses with a silk scarf, a pair of pearls or maybe even a nice pair of earrings. I think Jackie O would approve.

154. **Improve Your Mood with Music.** Music has a profound effect on most people's mood. It can lift us, enlighten us, cheer us up, and even help us maintain a certain mood. If you need joy in your life you can always find some kind of music to help with that. If you need a rush, a favorite boogie-woogie might be the answer. Besides being a marvelous source of pampering pleasures and an entertaining diversion, music can be a great restorative element in your life. Hospitals use music to help heal people, Patients are able

to relax and it provides total body response, including increasing the will to live in patients. How long has it been since you've really listened to the music that moves you and speaks to the depths of your soul? Take a few moments to listen to the many songs of your favorite music just as you would soak into a warm bath. Become saturated by the melodies and cleaned by the sounds - you'll emerge restored.

Get In a Good Mood

Do you ever just have those moments when you feel nice, relaxed, and happy with your life? That's how your 'me-time rituals should make you feel. Here are a few suggestions that will quietly get you in a good mood:

- ❖ Watch a movie where people fall in love.
- ❖ Realize the feeling you felt when you fell in love.
- ❖ Sleep peacefully during a rainy day.
- ❖ Quietly fall asleep in the arms of your lover.
- ❖ Watch your lover sleep in the middle of the night.
- ❖ Remember the moment before and after intimacy.
- ❖ Everyday look in the mirror and see a beautiful woman.
- ❖ Spend time thinking of these things that made you laugh.
- ❖ Hear a classic song on the radio.
- ❖ Listen to favorite musical CD.
- ❖ Listen to your children's laughter.
- ❖ Do your favorite things … things that make you happy.
- ❖ Reminisce about your best travel experience.

- ❖ Quietly eat your favorite foods.
- ❖ Buy that pair of new shoes you've always wanted.

  And a hundred other creative things!

Had we not loved ourselves at all, we could never have been obliged to love anything. So that self-love is the basis of all love. To love oneself is to live!

19

Enjoy Pampering Away From Home

In this chapter you will discover places to go that will give you great pampering experiences.

N
ow that you know how to host a 'Girls Night In' Pampering Party let's discuss some retreats away from home with wonderful spa possibilities. There is an overwhelming variety of spa types, but to help you find one that best suites you. I've divided the spas into simple categories, but first you'll need to answer a few questions.

1. What are your spa goals?
2. Are you visiting a spa to be pampered, to be cured, to find peace or to get fit?
3. Maybe you are looking for a romantic, once-in-a-lifetime with no-expense-spared-dream-holiday-kind-of-spa?

Hopefully you will find a bit of all those in one spa visit and you'll get an idea of how to figure out what kind you want by reading this section of he book. Here's a look at each away from home spa type.

Health Spas are residential establishments wholly dedicated to the pursuit of health, beauty and well being in all its forms.

It includes traditional health farms, new age holistic retreats, medical clinics and natural spas based around a natural source of mineral, thermal or seawater.

This kind of spa is usually located in a peaceful or picturesque surrounding. The health spa is a retreat as much as a healthy venue. An informal, relaxed atmosphere prevails and you can expect to spend much of your day in a robe being cared for by highly trained therapists with a high staff to guest ratio.

All food will be healthy, if not calorie controlled, often offering organic, vegetarian or menus catering for special dietary requirements.

As well as a large range of face and body treatments, health spas offer a full timetable of consultations, activities, classes, talks and demonstrations. Many spas offer specific weeklong health program for a varied range of targets from detoxing and relaxation to weight loss and quitting smoking. Ideal for true relaxation, detox plans, specific well-being programs, life changes, spiritual retreats, medical help, rest and post-operative recuperation. There are usually no bar, children, smoking, mobile phones, or conference facilities. Most health spas would not suit people who don't like staying in one place all the time.

Day Spas offer hourly services. Choose a day spa near your home or while traveling when you want a spa experience for a short period of time. Day spas are designed to provide a beautifying, relaxing, or pampering experience with individual treatments that last for as little as an hour or multiple treatments that may take up to a whole day.

Day spas are freestanding or located in health clubs, hotels, shopping centers, department stores, or even airports. A day center wholly dedicated to the pursuit of health, beauty and well-being. It includes any day center, including hair and beauty salons, complimentary health centers and wellness clinics and offers at least one hydrotherapy treatment. Varies from anything between a clinical, white-walled atmosphere geared towards walk-in appointments, to a subterranean, peaceful sanctuary geared towards pampering. This is a solitary experience where the only person you encounter is your therapist.

Most day spas will offer a large range of pampering and grooming treatments including massages, facials, pedicures, manicures and a wet room offering hydrotherapy treatments such as body wraps and balneotherapy. Inch-loss and toning treatments are also common. Beauty salons sometimes offer more specific anti-aging treatments such as laser therapy and face peels. Complimentary and well-being centers will offer a range of holistic, alternative, naturopathic or complimentary therapies. Try well-being in bite-size pieces. It's perfect for those who don't have the time or funds to go on a proper spa holiday but still want to de-stress, pamper themselves, maintain a sense of well-being, look after their skin, treat minor ailments, lose a few inches or just get-away from the hustle and bustle of normal life for an afternoon. If you're looking for activities

City Hotel/Urban Spas are found in city hotels. Choose a City Hotel, also called Urban Spa, when you are traveling or wish to have a day spa experience with hotel amenities like a health club and a restaurant. Steam rooms, saunas, pools, exercise equipment, and fitness classes may also be offered. Located in metropolitan hotels, some of these spas are open only to hotel guests, while others are accessible to the general public.

A hotel with a spa attached. Includes any residential venue whose primary purpose is accommodation rather than well-being - hotels, resorts, all-inclusive holiday villages, country clubs and inns - and also offers spa facilities. You share the hotel with people and families who are on holiday or even on work trips, which means relaxing in robes is restricted to your bedroom and the spa area only.

However, there is more freedom in terms of how you spend your time - you don't have to follow a program of activities and there is no restriction on smoking or drinking. By the same token, the staff to guest ratio is lower and there is usually no medical or health counseling service available. Hotel spas generally offer a good range of body and face treatments as well as a few studio classes per day, the quantity and choice of which varies between venues so check before you go. Holiday villages and resorts usually offer an unrivalled selection of sporting activities such as water sports, cycling, tennis and golf. Great for those who want to mix spa treatments with tourism, sports, entertainment or even work. It's ideal for those who want to pamper themselves without leaving the outside world. If you need support from staff to get healthy, this isn't the place for you. Also, you won't find as much peace and quiet here and you'll have to look presentable most of the time, as fellow residents won't be in spa mode.

Club Spas are a fitness location with spa facilities. Usually member's only. Includes any health club, gym or leisure centers offering a spa area. The spa is usually a sanctuary away from the action of the fitness area offering an environment similar to that of a regular day spa.

However, as those around you are regular visitors of the club, there is an opportunity to find friends and meet like-minded people.

On top of the fitness facilities offered by the health club, the salon area of the spa will offer similar treatments to a regular day spa. In addition, Club Spas are more likely to offer a swimming pool and a sauna or steam room. It's ideal for those who want to add spa treatments to their daily health and fitness regime. It's also great if you don't want to be bound to a monthly fee.

Cruise Spas are on a cruise ship with a spa center. A bit like staying at a hotel but more relaxed as everyone around you is on holiday - so no suits in sight. And even though there is a busy timetable of dinners, activities, games and entertainment, it is a good getaway in terms of leaving telephones, computers, cars and crowds behind. Spas are modern and well equipped, offering a good range of treatments. However, as food and drink is unrestricted, your cruise may swing wildly between bouts of culinary over-indulgence followed by recovery sessions at the spa. The salon area of the spa will offer similar treatments to a regular day spa. There will also usually be a gym and fitness studio offering a range of classes as well as a pool and saunas or steam room. A great way to get away from things and finding a sense of well-being while being entertained and pampered. If you feel trapped or claustrophobic on a ship this may not be a good one. If you want to lose weight - as food is included in the price of the holiday, bountiful and served buffet-style, it's hard not to over eat.

Destination Spas are for women who come to focus purposefully on lifestyle improvement, health enhancement, and self-renewal. Choose a Destination Spa if you seek total immersion in everything spa. Destination spas are places to go for a few days, a week, or even longer to enjoy the spa experience in the company of like-minded people. At these inspiring retreats, you find all-inclusive programs that integrate fitness, spa treatments, healthful cuisine, and lifestyle education.

Resort Spas are found in resort settings. Choose a Resort Spa if you want to combine a wide variety of recreational activities with a renewing spa experience. At these vacation resorts, spa treatments and services complement such activities as golf, tennis, horseback riding, skiing, and water sports. Healthful spa cuisine is on the menu alongside traditional fare, and alcohol is available. In the evening, guests can enjoy resort pastimes such as dancing and live entertainment. Children's programs may also be offered.

Pampering Spas nurtures the mind and body using soothing and indulgent treatments. A wide range of facials, manicures, pedicures, massages, tanning, hair grooming as well as a good range of fitness facilities such as a gym, studio and pool. Nothing is strenuous and everything is designed to make you feel nurtured. Great if you're stressed out and in need of some tender, loving care. If you want to be gently exercised then preened and primped, slathered in oils and massaged, and finally wrapped in fluffy white towels.

Therapeutic Spas cures an ailment of the mind or body and includes thalassotherapy spas, mineral water springs and medical clinics. There is a medical slant on all these treatments whether it is the minerals in the water that cure arthritis or foetal injections that bring back a bloom of youth. Pampering may not always be a priority, but you can be assured that the treatments you receive are first class and often proven to be effective in clinical trials. Try the therapeutic spa if you are physically run down or weak, if you need a cure for arthritis or dermatitis, if you are trying to quit smoking or drinking, if you are recovering from an operation, if you are looking for cosmetic surgery, or if you want to experience the current Renaissance of the European Spas.

Holistic Spas treats the whole body and mind to increase a sense of well-being. Holistic treatments maintain that beauty comes from within and that your health is a reflection of your mental state. The emphasis is therefore on spiritual fitness rather than physical fitness. Expect meditation to start your day, followed by Tai Chi or Yoga and then an Ayurvedic massage with a real fruit facial. Some holistic spas offer creative workshops and group healing sessions. Food will be organic or vegetarian and there will be a ban on toxins. This one is great if you are already interested in or curious about alternative therapies. If you are trying to find yourself, get in touch with nature or wanting to heal your soul after emotional upheavals.

Activity Spas offer a wide range of fitness and sporting activities or excels in one. Includes health clubs and fitness centers. You can find a spa that will cater for most activities: golf is a universal sport and common at spas around the world, horse riding is popular at America spas, cycling and trekking at European spas, and water sports at beach side resorts. Look hard enough and you can find spas that will cater to more obscure activities such as dance, martial arts or archery. If you want to get fit and lose weight but find treadmills boring. Great for those who want to develop a new sport or one that you have long-neglected. If you want to be outside and feel the blood pump around your veins this one is great. Often suitable for family holidays and couples.

Medical Spas focus on wellness and preventive healthcare or cosmetic and aesthetic procedures. Choose a Medical Spa if you are interested in healthcare in a spa setting, either at a day spa or at a spa with overnight accommodations. Medical spas offer traditional and complementary medical services supervised or administered by medical professionals. The spa's specialty may be diagnostic testing, preventive care, cosmetic procedures, or a combination of these.

Connoisseur Spas are the world's crème de la crème. Choose a Connoisseur Spa if you wish to experience the very best the spa world has to offer. These spas have been specially selected for their extraordinary ambience, luxurious accommodations, high staff-to-guest ratio, exceptional spa services, outstanding cuisine, and awards for excellence. Imagine a two person massage, fresh rose petals in your bath, a personal servant to carry your towel, your own bathrobe and sandals to keep, breathtaking bedroom views, outstanding spa cuisine by a world-renown chef, five-star room service...imagine heaven on earth and you are imaging a deluxe spa. For a romantic break, honeymoon or once in a lifetime holiday. To be treated like the most important person in the world. This is the best one if you want try the latest of everything and to catch a glimpse of celebrities.

Our first and last love is self-love.

~ Christian Nestell Bovee

20

Benefits of Spa Treatments

S pas were previously enjoyed only by the rich and famous at exclusive destination spas; now affordably priced these various treatments can help purge toxins from the body and mind. Proven to reduce inches from the waist and thighs. These treatments leave the body looking and feeling years younger.

When was the last time you were treated like a Queen? If you decide to visit a spa you'll definitely be treated like one. Spas are like hair and nail salons, only better. In addition to hair and nail services they offer relaxing muscle massages, pedicures, manicures, deep cleansing facials and eve body scrubs all in a comforting and soothing environment.

Winter wrecks havoc on our skin, especially our hands and feet leaving them dry, cracked and itching. Dead skin on your body can leave your skin so dry that oils and lotions have a hard time getting in, leaving you with a bad case of winter itch.

Every maturing woman should get a facial. A good facial will clean your pores, remove blackheads, acne, hair and even shaving bumps, leaving your face feel smooth and hydrated.

Massages can be purchased by the hour, (full body) or half hour (the back only). During a massage you will be asked to remove all your clothes. Don't be shy, but feel free to leave your underwear on. A sheet will cover you at all times. So lay back enjoy the candlelight and listen to smooth sounds, while being massaged with warm oils.

Listed are the different types of massage treatments and the benefits of each. I hope this will help you make a decision as to what kind of massage you would like to choose.

Aromatherapy uses essential oils that are derived from various plant sources. The oils are massaged, inhaled or used in baths to "therapeutically" affect the individual's physical and mental well being. **Benefits**: Specific blends of oils will stimulate, balance or relax mental responses, and aid in circulatory, muscular and respiratory functions.

Ayurveda teaches that the foundation of all material life can be identified in terms of the elements; earth, fire, water, wind and air. All disease according to Ayurveda is triggered by disturbances in one's equilibrium. These disturbances may be caused by external, internal, physical or psychological factors.
Benefits: This holistic approach to well being is believed to slow the ageing process and improve the quality of life.

Body Polishes, Scrubs and Glows use natural pastes made from substances such as sea salt, apricot kernels and sugar to exfoliate the skin. A hydrotherapy component can be used to rinse off the product, and is followed by an aromatherapy or Swedish massage.

Benefits: Any of these treatments promote the flow of nutrient-rich circulation and hydrate the skin.

Body Wraps have been used for centuries to promote the release of toxins through sweat and improve the metabolism. The original herbal wrap used natural linen sheets, soaked in therapeutic herbs, which were wrapped snugly around the body. Many body wraps today include an application of warmed substances such as seaweed or mud, applied to the body as a mask. Then the client is wrapped in pampering blankets.

Benefits: Wraps aid in detoxification and relaxation, and leave the skin hydrated.

Facials are treatments directed at enhancing the quality of your skin. A skin analysis precedes the service to determine the best treatment to cleanse, soothe, hydrate and rejuvenate the skin. Many of these services include facial massage and revitalizing masks.

Benefits: Treatments result in a cleaner, better hydrated and rejuvenated skin.

Hot Stone Massage is a healing therapy using warmed, smooth volcanic stones to massage the body.

Benefits: It provides a warm penetrating heat. It is deeply relaxing.

Hydrotherapy is an age-old healing method used in spas around the world, and as the name suggests, is the use of water in treatments. Water's greatest healing attribute is its ability to hold temperatures, both hot and cold. Medical and Holistic physicians have long recognized the benefits of water, often recommending heating blankets, hot baths and cold packs to reduce pain and inflammation in muscles and joints. Spas feature hydrotherapy in many very enjoyable, specialized treatments such as the Hydrotherapy Bath Tub, Vichy Shower, Swiss Shower, Blitz Guss (Scotch Hose), Thalassotherapy and more. Hydrotherapy bath treatments are performed in state-of-the-art bath equipment, often combining water and air jets. An underwater massage wand is used, and specialized lymphatic drainage treatments can also be administered in the Hydrotherapy Bath. Natural herbal oils, salts, mud or algae are added to the bath to rejuvenate and relax.
Benefits: Hydrotherapy baths relieve muscular tension and improve circulation.

Lomi Oluli is a Hawaiian bodywork method. The therapist provides a flowing massage to align the body, mind and spirit.
Benefits: This returns clients to a peaceful and balanced state.

Lymphatic Drainage Massage massage technique using gentle pressure to activate the lymphatic system, which is the body's immune system. Treatments can be performed utilizing underwater wand techniques.
Benefits: This treatment can reduce edema (fluid retention), and aid in detoxification as it soothes and relaxes the body.

Parafango is a mixture of different forms of mud and paraffin that is pampering and applied to the body. The client is then wrapped in pampering blankets.

Benefits: Parafango wraps ease aches and pains in muscles and joints and nourishes, soothes and hydrates the skin.

Reflexology applies pressure points on specific areas of the feet and hands that correspond to areas throughout the body.

Benefits: Not only is this a treat for both hands and feet, it's deeply relaxing, and provides an overall tonic for the body as the reflex points release energy blockages in corresponding areas of the body.

Reiki is Japanese for "universal life energy". This is a laying of hands therapy based on the theory that life force energy flows through us, bringing vitality.

Benefits: This creates balance, harmony and a sense of well-being.

Scotch Hose is a strong stream of water pressure applied from the feet to the back and shoulders. This treatment is most effective when both hot and cold applications of water are used. Benefits: This is an excellent "wake-up" tonic for the body and promotes the flow of circulation.

Shiatsu is an oriental method of massage using acupressure points applied to the whole body.

Benefits: It improves energy flow and balances the body.

Swedish Massage consists of a combination of "hands on" techniques usually applied by Registered Massage Therapists. Various strokes are used to relax tension in muscles and relieve pain. Registered Massage Therapists in Ontario are taught to assist in recovery from neuromuscular conditions, whiplash, motor vehicle accidents, surgeries, and pregnancy discomforts.

Benefits: This massage relieves muscular pain and tension, improves circulation, and many physicians are prescribing it to reduce stress-related illnesses and conditions. (Many extended health insurance plans provide reimbursement when receipts are submitted.)

Swiss Shower is a powerful massage using multiple jets of water pressure in the privacy of a shower. It is usually taken in combination with Body Polishes and Body Wraps.

Benefits: This invigorating water therapy relieves muscular tension and improves circulation. It is both restorative and relaxing, and rinses the body following scrubs and wraps.

Thai Massage is performed on a floor mat with the client fully clothed. It incorporates aspects of reflexology, acupressure, shiatsu and yoga to trigger the flow of energy throughout the body.

Benefits: This treatment mobilizes all the joints and muscles throughout the body.

Thalassotherapy uses seawater or algae (sea plants) in treatments such as Body Wraps and Hydrotherapy to benefit the skin and circulation.

"Thalasso" is the Greek word for "sea" and these treatments are particularly popular along France's Brittany Coast.

Benefits: Thalassotherapy is used to relieve arthritic aches and pains, soothe the skin and revitalize the body.

Vichy Shower is a horizontal rain-bar with numerous showerheads positioned above a wet-table on which the client receives treatment. This light waterfall is used to relax and cleanse treatment products off the body.

Benefits: The use of different temperatures and pressure of water stimulates circulation. This is a deeply relaxing therapy.

All life is an experiment. The more experiments you make the better
~ Ralph Waldo Emerson

Conclusion

Your body is your temple. Treat it as such.
It's the only one you have and there's no true replacement.

I n Greek Mythology, Venus's name is Aphrodite. She is known as the Daughter of Heaven and Sea, the child of Uranus and Gaia. Her story tells of fertility, love and pleasure.

Venus wasn't conceived out of pleasure, but she worked hard to find her own. She was born when Gaia, Goddess of Mother Earth, got so angry at her husband Uranus that she sliced off his genitals and threw them into the sea. They mixed with the foam of the ocean and formed Venus, a symbol unconcerned with maternal issues and focused on sensuality and pleasure.

Venus married and bore children. The goddess loved to pamper herself and cultivate her beauty. Her symbol represents the hand-held mirror that Venus used to admire her beauty. Truly, Venus has become the symbol for pampering of a woman.

Pampering Is a Woman's Thing

Indulging in pampering pleasures is a lifestyle. Choosing to add delight, comfort, and joy to each day doesn't have to stop when your life gets better, when you get the dream job, when you get the new car, the new home or more money. Pampering pleasures are a woman's way to indulge in soothing-self-love and 'me-time ritual's. It's a daily process to help her take care of herself.

Integrating innocent pleasures into your daily living brings change, energy and inner renewal. You view the world differently and notice things you might otherwise have overlooked. Implement as many pampering pleasures as you can in your daily life. You can do them for a day or a week or even longer. It's up to you! As you think of new treats, why not add them to this book. Once you do, you'll look forward to beautiful bit and pieces of pampering each day.

It is my wish that these pampering pleasures will transform your life. Allow them to enrich your days, ease your mind, lift your spirits, enhance your body, and rejuvenate your soul.

Know thyself.
To know is to be intimately acquainted or familiar with.
You should be your own best expert.

About The Author

Ella is the author of several published books: *Will The Real Women Please Stand Up!, 1001 Reasons To Think Positive; Heated Pleasures: A Modern Woman's Guide To Heating Up Your Sex Life; Relationship Quickies; Pampering Pleasures; and Moving In The Right Direction.* She is a professional ghostwriter, experienced sex educator, and motivational speaker.

Her books have been featured on hundreds of radio and TV shows throughout the United States, Canada, Europe, Japan and China. Ella is a pioneer and leader in the field of women's issues, women's studies, and innovative management and is known across the world as a motivator, educator and one of the most knowledgeable teachers in the area of personal success and self-esteem.

Ella conducts women based seminars and workshops for groups and organizations throughout the country. She has also written numerous articles and essays that have helped millions of women improve their quality of life. An educator for more than 30 years she has appeared on numerous daytime talk shows, and CNN Airport News. Her work has appeared in major newspapers and magazines and journals, including *The New York Times, The Dallas Morning News, The St. Louis Post Dispatch, Chicago Sun Times, Philadelphia Enquirer, Miami Herald, Boston Globe, Cosmopolitan, Success Magazine* and many others.

She is a member American Society of Journalist and Authors (ASJA), Texas Auto Writers Association (TAWA) and Global One Auto Writers

(GOAW). She is President of Knowledge Concepts Publishers; Editor-in-chief of Global One Magazine; and Publisher of Global One Travel and Automotive Newspaper in DeSoto, Texas. Ella Patterson is available for media interviews, book signings and speaking engagements. She lives outside Dallas, Texas with her husband Martin and their two dog; Cash and Mo'ney.

She can be reached at **ellampatterson@aol.com**
Call 972-854-1824 or fax: 214-988-2867

Appendix A

Meanings of Candle Colors

WHITE: Self; Protection; Purification; Purity; Innocence; Centering; Truth; Sincerity; Meditation; Peace; Power of a Higher Nature; Greater Attainments in Life; Spirituality.

RED: Protection; Strength; Blood; Passion; Courage; Health; Power; Fire Elemental; Sexuality; Vigor; Energy; Enthusiasm; Will Power; To conquer fear or laziness.

Light BLUE: Healing; Patience; Happiness; Quests; Intuition; Opportunity; Tranquility; Understanding. Safe Journey; Harmony; Peace.

DARK BLUE: The Goddess; West; Water Elemental; Inspiration; Truth; Dreams; Protection; Change; Impulse; Fidelity; Deep Emotion; Peace; Meditation; Changeability;

GREEN: Money; Fertility; Growth; Employment; Luck; Healing; Balance; Prosperity; Courage; Garden blessing; Abundance; Generosity; Renewal; Marriage.

YELLOW: Air Elemental; Intellect; Creative Work; Learning; Changes; Confidence; Attraction; Harmony; Clairvoyance; Charm; Imagination; Power of the Mind; Gentle persuasion; Action.

BROWN: Animal Health; Endurance; Steadiness; Houses & Homes; Physical Objects; Overcoming uncertainty and hesitancy; Money and Financial Success; Concentration; Intuition; Study.

PINK: Love; Peace; Femininity; Friendship; Honor; Morality; Emotional Love; Affection; Romance; Spiritual Awakening; Healing of the Spirit; Togetherness.

ORANGE: God; Attraction; Stimulation; Energy; Healing; Vitality; Encouragement; Adaptability; Luck; Clearing the Mind; Dominance, Sudden Changes; Change Luck.

PURPLE: Power; Dignity; Spiritual Development; Meditation, Spirituality; Intuition; Ambition; Spirit Communication; Tension; Business Progress; Healing Severe Diseases; Success; Idealism;

GOLD: The God; Solar Energy; Physical Strength; Power; Success; Mental Growth; Skill Sought; Healing Energy; Fortune; Divination; Creative Work; Intuition; Money; Fast Luck; Attracts Higher Influences.

SILVER: The Goddess; Lunar magic; Removes negative forces; Opens astral gates; Conducts Energy; Meditation; Creative Work; Protection; Money; Success; Balance.

VIOLET: Self Improvement; Intuition; Success in searches; Creative Work.

BLACK: Endings; Closing of Doors; Protection; Truth; Remove Discord or Confusion; Releasing

GREENISH-YELLOW: To Negate; Discord, Sickness, Anger, Jealousy, Cowardice, Anger.

INDIGO: Meditation; Spirit Communication; Karma Working; Balance; Learn the Ancient Wisdom;

GRAY: Vision Quests; Veiling; Cancellation; Hesitation; Competition.

LAVENDER: Spiritual Development; Psychic Growth; Divination; Blessings.

MAGENTA: Usually burned with other candles; Quick Change; Spiritual Healing,

Index

ceramic vaporizers, 51
chamomile, 49
chamomile tea, 93
champagne, 94, 95, 97
champagne bath, 95
charms, 49
cheesecloth, 85
chemical peels, 87
chest, 64, 72, 73, 93, 95
chic-flick, 164
children's programs, 188
chilled bottle of champagne, 95
chilled wine, 123
chipping, 149
chiseled stone, 117
chocolate, 122, 142, 166, 167
choose a city hotel, also called urban spa, 186
church, 41, 61, 171
cigarette smoke, 74
cinnamon, 95
city spas, 186
claustrophobic, 188
clay, 51
clay rings, 52
cleansers, 87
club spas, 187
cluttered, 110
coffee, 30, 35, 141, 142, 143, 158, 165, 166, 171
cold cuts, 97
cold packs, 195
cold soaks, 77
cold water baths, 96
collection of antidotes, 24
comfortable chair, 30, 31, 108
communicate, 70
communication, 38
completeness, 28
computer desk, 30

computers, 105, 187
concentrated oils, 50
concentration, 32
condoms, 124
congested nose remedy, 52
congestion, 51
connoisseur spa, 191
conversations, 120
cool cotton sheets, 109
corked bottle, 51
cosmetics, 49
cotton balls, 46
couch, 30
country clubs, 186
creating sensual ambience, 107
crowds, 187
cruise spas, 187
cucumber mint soak, 81
cucumbers, 66
Cupping, 99
cuticles, 78, 79, 81, 149
cycling, 186
cypress, 52

D

daily pampering, 156
day spa treatments, 185
day spas, 99, 185
decorate your special place, 31
deep belly breathing, 93
definition
    spa treatments, 193
department store spas, 185
department stores, 146
destination spas, 188
deterioration of essential oils, 51
detoxification, 85, 194, 195
detoxify, 84
detoxifying, 52

pollutants, 87
pollution, 74
pools, 186
popcorn, 169
potpourri, flowers, 111
preparing for massage, 63
pressure points, 196
private places to relax, 29
private sanctuaries, 121
private sanctuary, 114
professional athlete, 90
professional athletes, 24
props and supplies, 124
protecting your face, 74
public park, 139
pumice stick, 159
pumice stone, 96
putting the tips into practice, 28

Q

quiet corner of a room, 30
quiet ride, 39
quiet spot, 166
quiet surroundings, 72
quiet times, 29

R

radio, 36
radios, 105
razor blade, 147
read, 3, 28, 29, 30, 32, 36, 57,
63, 101, 120, 141, 142, 152,
154, 158, 162, 165, 166, 178
read newspapers, 36
read this book, 3, 28
reading bedrooms, 120
recliner, 30
reenergize, 30
reflexology, 197

Reflexology, 99
refresh your spirit, 29
refrigerator, 121
regroup,, 30
rejuvenation, 22
relax, 29, 30, 32, 86, 89, 91, 93,
99, 100, 109, 113, 193, 195,
197, 198
Relax, 71, 88, 93
relax your body, 32
relaxing, 29, 52
relaxing baths, 93
remove, dead skin, 82
removing dead cells, 76
renew my spirits, 139
resort spas, 186, 188
restaurant, 186
resting wrap, 78, 90
restorative properties, 49
restoring your body, 78
rethink, 30
retreat, 29, 91, 105, 106, 112,
121, 184
revitalize, 30, 112, 198
reviving, 52
reward yourself, 170
ringing telephones, 30
rituals, 70
robe, 47
rose, 51
rosemary, 49
rosemary infused water, 90
Rosemary oil, 89
roses, 139
rough heels, 152
rubber bristles, 46
rubber gloves, 145
Russian banyas, 70

S

watch television, 36
water, 70, 71, 76, 77, 78, 85,
88, 89, 90, 91, 92, 93, 95, 96,
98, 108, 186, 188, 189, 190,
193, 195, 196, 197, 198
water sports, 186
wearing headphones, 38
welcome door color, 104
wellness clinics, 185
what a woman wants, 22
whiplash, 197
whipped cream, 166
wholesomeness, 31
why a book on sensuous
healing, 1
window box, 31
window treatments, 116

wine, 97
wine, champagne and shrimp,
97
woman's heat, 27

Y

yearbooks, 177
Yoga, 189
your favorite drink, 31
your special space, 30, 31, 32

Z

Zen bathing, 91
zest, 107

Ella Patterson

Audiotapes, Videos, and Books

By Ella Patterson

Audiotapes

Higher Expectations (10 audio tapes)

Enjoy Ella's humor, compassion and simple wisdom as she presents her complete success program on tape. In this insightful and entertaining series for both adult and young adult, Ella shares how people can enhance and tune up their lives, by improving their emotional, spiritual and professional lives.

Videos: Ella Patterson's Girls Night Out

Other Books

- ❖ Will The Real Women Please Stand Up: A woman's guide to female sexuality and self esteem
- ❖ 1001 Reasons To Think Positive: Special Insights, Tips and Techniques for achieving a better life
- ❖ Successful Things That Successful Women Do
- ❖ Stupid Things Men Should Never Say To Women
- ❖ Will The Real Men Please Stand Up: A man's guide to incorporating romance and passion in his relationships

To order any of Ella's books, audiotapes and videos please call 972-854-1984

Acknowledgments

This book has not only helped me understand the need to be pampered, it has shown me that every woman needs to indulge in easy fun filled pampering techniques. I attribute experiences gained during the writing of this book to many individuals. They have allowed me tremendous freedom of speech. Without their faith in me I wouldn't have been challenged to dig so deeply for wonderful pampering pleasures. I'd like to take this time to say thanks to each of them. They are my angels. My warmest thanks to these dear friends who shared their hearts, souls, pampering activities, fantasies, desires and stories with me. Without their knowledge and experiences this book would not exist.

I owe my most spirited thanks to my children, Juanna, T'Juanna and Martin III. Juanna you are the oldest; I'm depending on you to guide and set an example for the other two. T'Juanna, my kindest and most attention getting child, remember to stay alert and enjoy life while you're working to reach your goals. Martin you are the youngest, yet you are the strongest and the most understanding; watch over your sisters and keep in touch with them more often. I adore and love each of you.

Martin Patterson, my warmest thanks and undying love for being there every step of the way. You spoil me daily with pampering pleasures.

To Fletcher Ollie, one of my dearest friends; thanks for the eternal friendship and for watching my back. You taught me patience.

To Robert Corley, thanks for helping me bring this book to life and most of all for being my rock. Every woman needs a rock like you. You have taught me how to accept pampering. I am forever grateful for your pampering skills.

To Coach Edmond Peters, the pampering began with you about thirty years ago. You taught me the meaning of real pampering and to you I am forever grateful. You taught me how to be a pampered lady.

To Walter Humphrey, my brother and friend. May God keep his hands on you and may you soon receive the pampering pleasures you so deserve.

To Marva Houston thanks for never slacking on our friendship.

To Brenda Brown, special thanks for helping me keep my stock up; girllllll you were so right!

To Denella Braxton, I am ever grateful for the long talks and laughter during our late night phone calls.

To Bettie Artis, you saved my spirit. We are the same in so many ways.

To Lauren Freeman, if only there was enough time for us to bond. We are sisters in spirit.

To my brother, Herbert Jones, who taught me what it *really* means to have someone stick by you when times get rough. Thanks for the constant and everlasting support in all I do. I love you dearly.

To Jan Miller thank you for your professionalism, competence, and suggestions on many of my projects. Your leadership and tenacity have helped me grasp the insight needed to complete this project. To your wonderful staff who has always been professional, courteous, helpful, and on the mark when I needed guidance of how to bring my manuscripts to book form. Thanks a bunch!

My God in heaven, you gave me the fortitude and know-how to complete this project so that I may assist women all over the world and help them feel better about themselves. I have been so blessed. Continue to keep your hands on me and your arms wrapped around me. I need you always.

Space For Your Private Notes

Pampering Pleasures

Pampering Pleasures

■ *Books by Ella*

 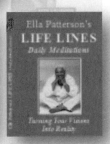 

Order Form

For more information on Global One Systems or any Ella Patterson products, call 972-765-1950 or send in the coupon below.

Return To: Global One Systems, Inc (GOES)

P.O. Box 973 Cedar Hill, Texas 75106 or phone 972-223-1558

Please send me information on Global One Systems books, lectures, seminars or products.

NAME (please print) _____

PHONE _____

ADDRESS _____

CITY _____

STATE _____ ZIP _____

Please use ballpoint pen only

❑   ___ Pampering Pleasures - $14.95 ea.

❑   ___ Will The Real Women Please Stand Up! - $14.95 ea.

❑   ___ Will The Real **MEN** Please Stand Up! - $19.95 ea.

❑   ___ Moving In The Right Direction - $14.95 ea.

❑   ___ Stupid Things Men Should Never Say - $10.00 ea.

❑   ___ Heated Pleasures - $15.95 ea.

❑   ___ Sexual Healing $14.95 ea.

Email: ellampatterson@aol.com   /   Website: ellapatterson.com